Scams, Scams, Scams, and More Scams

Roberta Lydick

ISBN 979-8-89601-642-7 (paperback)
ISBN 979-8-89601-643-4 (digital)

Hawes & Jenkins Publishing
Meadville, PA
www.hawesjenkins.com

Printed in the United States of America

To my immediate family and my dear friend Betty, who has been with me during this newest endeavor in my life. Thank you all for guiding me and always being here with me!

I would like to thank both peer groups for helping all people who have been through bad experiences with identity thieves who stole good people's identities and used celebrities' personal pictures to victimize unsuspecting people out of their money and have them lose trust. Losing trust is the most horrific thing to lose. It is hard to be able to trust again, and everyone needs to work hard to gain that trust back!

Both groups help with all types of scams in the world, not just specific scams, and all is held confidential!

Here is one organization!

FightCybercrime.org and our peer support group is called The Cybercrime Support Group. The peer support group is for those who have experienced:

Romance Fraud,
Romance Fraud with Crypto Investment Fraud and
Crypto Investment Fraud

This is the second group that helps.

This is the other group that helps all, and they know from personal experience how it feels to be a scam victim. You do not realize how many victims are out there until you start talking and getting to know people.

God bless them all!

Author's Note: Any emails correspondence scams I had received are true and left unedited. Their grammar is very bad, as you will see, and I never clicked on any links replied back to them. All written capitalization or punctuation are just like they write. My experience was horrific. Everyone needs education on how to not fall prey to these scammers.

INTRODUCTION

Many of the scams listed are what I receive, and probably many others, in their daily emails.

A scammer knows he is a scammer, so there is no point in telling him. Your time is valuable. Respect yourself, learn, and move on. Your healing comes first. Do not "play" with scammers. Attention keeps the scam alive.

The longer you talk, the more chances they get to lie, guilt you, and pull you back in.

They may even try to hack your account and use your profile to scam others.

Based on data from 2025, Pakistan, Tanzania, India, Nigeria, and Indonesia have the highest rates of fraud, largely due to a lack of protective safeguards. Conversely, the US is the most targeted country for scams, followed by the UK, Canada, India, and Australia. Turkey is identified as a major hub for mobile Trojan banking malware, often targeting Western nations. The highest fraud rates are in Pakistan, Tanzania, India, Nigeria, and Indonesia, which are noted as having the lowest safeguards and highest rates of fraud in the 2025 Global Fraud Index. The United States leads the world in the number of scam victims, followed by the UK, Canada, India, and Australia. Turkey is a major leader in sophisticated mobile Trojan banking malware, targeting local users and Spain, Australia, and the United States. The most protected against fraud are Denmark, Finland, Norway, the Netherlands, and Luxembourg. These rankings show a divide between nations with high fraud origination due to weaker infrastructure.

Anyone who has been scammed and reported the scams is recommended to keep the app, along with all associated evidence, immediately after being scammed, but with specific caveats regarding security. Documentation—such as chat logs, transaction histories, usernames, and screenshots—is crucial for law enforcement, bank disputes, and investigations!

When you have been scammed, it is crucial to keep the platform, all correspondence, and any related documents, such as emails, text messages, and phone logs, to help law enforcement officers. This is your paper trail, and they need this all.

Banks, credit card companies, and payment platforms require proof of fraud to initiate chargebacks, dispute transactions, or reverse wire transfers. If reported as a scam to the FBI (IC3), the Federal Trade Commission (FTC), or local police, this evidence provides concrete leads—fraudulent phone numbers, email addresses, or account IDs—to track down the criminals. Reporting with evidence helps platforms identify, block, and shut down scammers' accounts, protecting other potential victims. If personal information was shared, these records help you document the breach and, if necessary, prove that fraudulent accounts were not created. Keep screenshots of all conversations, profiles, and fake websites. Save all transaction and payment records. Even if they are painful, don't delete messages!

Scams are the worst of the worst because they target victims who have already lost money to a scam. If you've experienced a scam, you might be next targeted by a refund or recovery scam. In these types of scams, you're told they can help get your money back or recover the prize or item you never got. The first thing they want you to do is pay a fee to recover what you lost or paid already. If you pay them, you'll lose more money again.

It does not make a difference if it's a refund scam promising to get your money back or a recovery scam claiming to get you the prize or products you were promised; the scheme usually follows a set pattern.

This is what happens if you already paid a scammer. Scammers buy a sucker list, which is personal information such as your name, address, phone number, type of scam, and how much you were scammed for. These lists are traded or sold, so be prepared to be contacted over and over again. Remember not to fall for the scam again.

They will contact you in all ways, including social media platforms, claiming to be identity thieves of the exact same person who originally scammed you. If it is a recovery scam, they know all about the type of scam you were involved in and how much you lost. They will tell you a fee for them to recover your stolen funds and find the perpetrators. They want to gain your trust and will say they work for a government or consumer advocate agency. Do not trust calls, letters, emails, texts, or messages from someone you don't know. Never pay upfront fees or give out personal information. Don't pay with gift cards, cryptocurrency, or wire transfers; do not pay with cash, Cash App, or deposit a check they sent. The check they send is fake, and it will be too late once you cash it and send money to them. You lose all! Remember to always research, don't click on links, say no, and report!

Report it to the FTC at ReportFraud.ftc.gov or to your state attorney general.

When you report these scammers, you help law enforcement stop them and alert others in your community to the scam.

META SUES ADVERTISERS OVER ALLEGED CELEBRITY IMPERSONATION SCAMS

On February 26, Meta is taking enforcement actions against accused scammers. They are blocking domain names of scammers' websites and closing down their accounts. The schemes are known as celeb bait, and they undermine the trust of people and violate Meta's policies. They gain personal information and get money sent to them. These are scammers who are impersonating celebrities to get money from victims. Lawmakers are calling on online platforms to do more to stop these scammers. A bill introduced in the US Senate would require platforms to take steps to stop fraudulent and deceptive ads. Around 16 percent of scam victims were reached by scammers on social media, 8 percent were reached by scammers using a digital marketplace, and 7 percent clicked on a fraudulent link.

REVERSE PHONE LOOKUP SCAM

If you are tired of receiving calls from strange numbers, there is a way to find out who is calling without paying a fee. You can search phone numbers linked to social platforms as well. With telemarketing and spam calls on the rise, it is more important than ever to have a reliable phone number lookup service that does all this without a fee. Being able to look up landline or mobile numbers can be useful for all to avoid scams or just try to find out who called you.

Services like Truecaller and Whitepages provide identification of phone numbers, or you can try Google phone number lookup for free by searching directly in Google. Social Catfish is different from these; it was built especially for online safety and scam prevention. Social Catfish combines both reverse phone lookup and verification tools, along with reverse image search, email verification, social media profile analysis, comprehensive background reports, and a real-time scam database.

Red flags are VoIP or virtual numbers being used; refusal to video chat or call; a number that does not match their story; multiple numbers or frequent changes; number lookup results linked to scam reports; beyond basic free number lookup searches; and trusting your instincts. Social Catfish goes over and above to check the number that's been messaging you. Free phone number lookup will tell you maybe where they are located and provide basic information. Social Catfish will do more than give basic information. Social Catfish is an all-in-one platform investigation, image verification technology, cross-platform identity matching, an active scam database, expert human support, and the smart choice for online safety.

Who owns a phone number—you deserve more than fragments of information. You need the complete picture, and that's exactly what Social Catfish delivers. Some services offer free cell phone number lookup. Truecaller, Whitepages, and FastPeopleSearch provide basic information without fees. Google search and social media platforms like Facebook also allow free number searches. For more comprehensive results, including hidden profiles and social media connections, Social Catfish offers detailed searches that go beyond basic free tools.

The best free cheater lookup by phone number options include Social Catfish's free trial, Spokeo, and BeenVerified, which search dating sites and social platforms. You can manually search for the number on Facebook, Instagram, Tinder, and other dating apps. Social Catfish specializes in uncovering hidden dating profiles and verifying if someone is using their phone number on cheating or hookup sites.

Truecaller, NumLookup, and Google search allow free number lookup with no charge and without registration. All you need to do is enter the phone number to see basic caller ID information, but these free tools have limitations. Social Catfish provides more thorough investigations, including social media links, email addresses, and dating profiles, while protecting your privacy.

Phone number lookup free no-sign-up options include NumLookup, FreeCarrierLookup, and searching directly on Google or social media platforms. These require no account creation and provide instant basic results. For deeper searches across multiple databases and dating sites without delays, Social Catfish streamlines the process with comprehensive reports in one search.

To look up a number for free with name, no charge, try reverse searching on Google by typing the number in quotes, checking Whitepages or FastPeopleSearch, or searching directly on Facebook and LinkedIn. You can also use Truecaller's app for caller identification. For complete results, including associated social media accounts and verified identities, Social Catfish combines multiple search methods in one comprehensive lookup.

In today's digital age, having a reliable phone number lookup service is essential. With the above-mentioned free services, you can easily identify unknown callers without having to spend any money. However, it's important to use these services responsibly and be aware of their limitations. Stay safe and informed with the help of these free phone number lookup services.

How a computer hacker infiltrated a phone scam operation, exposing fraudsters and their schemes:

ROBOCALL SCAMS

Automated calls from scammers do not stop. If you return any of the calls, you sometimes get a recording that the call is no longer in service. You might actually get a person who will answer the call. Just play along and try to record the conversation and activity on a Trojan horse setup to see if the call is a scam, and ten to one, it is a scam. Some people will try to get telephone scammers online and record the conversations; many post their encounters on YouTube. Talking to them actually provides proof that all they want is to scam you out of money. Age does not matter to these scammers, and they will tell you anything to get as much money from you as possible. They will say that you sound like their grandmother or that you don't sound your age. The best you can do is to keep the conversation going to waste their time, like they are wasting your time.

Some of the scammers call from India, and they will ask you to log in to your computer to gain access using a remote-access software program called TeamViewer. The developers of TeamViewer have discovered that criminals in India were abusing their software, so they temporarily banned its use from computers initiating connections from India. But it did not stop scammers from asking US and UK consumers to initiate access into computers in India. Tips to avoid these scams: be in charge at all times; do not let them gain access to any of your electronic devices; do not divulge personal information; and do not send money to them at all.

When answering the phone and it is not a live person but a recorded message, that is what robocalls are. When receiving a robocall, the call is generally trying to sell you something that is illegal. The only way the call is not illegal is if they have written consent from the company they are trying to sell something for. This is why robocalls are scams. It is cheap and easy for scammers to make these robocalls over the internet from anywhere in the world.

Scammers like to make robocalls claiming they are from government agencies calling about taxes, Medicare, or your Social Security number. They tell you that you owe money, and if you do not pay or give them personal information, they say you will be arrested. Also, never agree to wire money, pay with a gift card, use payment apps, or send bitcoins or other cryptocurrency. Those are methods scammers like to use, and there is always an urgent appeal. The government will never call; they will send letters through the mail. The same goes if you get a robocall for debt relief, car warranties, credit repair, or anything else.

You can use call-blocking to reduce robocalls. Scammers make it look as though the number from the Social Security Administration is legitimate. The best thing to do is hang up and call the Social Security office to ask if they are making robocalls, and give them the number and information from the robocall.

The best things to do when you hear a recorded message selling things: just hang up, block the phone number, and report it to the FTC and DoNotCall.gov. The FTC can track down the scammers behind the calls with the information you give them. The FTC takes the callers' numbers reported to them and releases them to the public. This helps phone companies working on call-blocking and helps law enforcement identify the scammers. Billions of calls have been stopped by reporting the numbers. The Do Not Call registry cannot stop all unwanted calls people get, but registering phone numbers can reduce the calls you receive.

OVERDUE TRAFFIC TICKET SCAM

Chances are, you have gotten a scam text about unpaid toll charges or know someone who has. Now scammers are going even further and pretending to be the Department of Motor Vehicles (DMV) from states all over the country. They insist that you pay for an "overdue traffic ticket" and threaten to suspend your driving privileges, among other things, if you do not. Here is how the scam works.

USPS TEXT SCAM

You receive a text message about a package coming via the United States Postal Service. The text might have confirmed your order, said a package is out for delivery, or said there's a problem, like unpaid postage, a missed delivery, or that you need to update your shipping preferences. The text will ask you to click a link to learn more or fix the problem. There's a very good chance the text message that says it's from USPS, or FedEx…or DHL is really from a scammer.

UNEXPECTED TEXT SCAM

Anytime people receive a text, they always open the text. There is a huge jump in reported fraud losses involving text scams; the FTC notes a study finding open rates can be as high as 98 percent. The scammers want you to respond to their messages, because all responses have them earn money. There are many ways you can keep your money safe. Don't give out your personal information. If you do, they use the information to steal your identity. Here's how you can increase your chances of keeping your money safe. If you get anything saying a new account was opened under your name, report it to IdentityTheft.

gov. They will ask you to freeze your credit at each of the three credit bureaus, check your credit report, and set up an IRS PIN.

TOLL TEXT SCAM

From monicabradley5802@outlook.com

Pennsylvania Department of Transportation
It is documented in our records that you have outstanding traffic citations that remain unpaid. Pursuant to 15-C-16.003 of the Pennsylvania Administrative Code, failure to remit full payment by March 18, 2026 will lead to following actions being imposed on you: 1. DMV violation system notification will be issued, 2. Your vehicle registration will be suspended starting March 20, 2026, 3. Your driving privileges will be suspended for 30 days, 4. Referral to a toll collection agency, which will add a 55% processing fee. Potential ramifications and harm to your credit score may also occur. Pay immediately: https://pa.com-red.cc/us To avoid license suspension and legal issues, you must settle the payment before enforcement begins. (Reply Y, reopen this message to click the link, or paste it into your browser.)

Reply from Senator's office:
From: Berta
Sent: Thursday, March 19, 2026 3:26 PM
To: Monica pahousegop.com>
Subject: [EXTERNAL]: Is this a scam?

Yes, it is
District Director to
State Representative J.D.K.
15th Legislative District

ACCIDENTAL TEXT MESSAGES

You get a text message asking if you are busy or saying they are running late from an unknown number not in your contacts. If you reply, then they apologize and ask if you are ever in their area, you can meet for coffee. Delete and block them. You can even text a screenshot to 7726. Once they receive the text, they ask for a number where the text came from.

ONLINE PHONE AND TEXT MESSAGE SCAM

Scammers will reach out to you and remind you of a promised political donation, will demand money, or threaten your safety or computer access. They ask you to scan a QR code or get cash cards to have the harassment stop.

Call 911 to report. Do not click on anything. If you think you owe money, go back to the original source and check to make sure.

GRANDPARENT SCAM

Please be aware of the grandparent scams. They call on the phone, and the scammer claims to be either your grandchild, law enforcement, or a lawyer. They scare you into thinking your grandchild is in custody for a crime or was in an accident.

The scammer may know some personal information about you and the grandchild, but usually uses a script that relies on your answers to fill in the blanks. To make the story seem more credible, the scammer sometimes puts someone else on the phone to portray a police officer, bail bondsman, or lawyer.

The scammer will pressure you for money needed for their bail or medical expenses. They will instruct you to go to your financial institution to withdraw cash and send it to an address through.

JOB OFFER TEXT SCAM

If it sounds too good to be true, it probably is, and most likely a scam. These texts promise jobs that pay highly, work from home at your own pace, or get paid to shop; they all sound great and are scams. The goal of the scammer is to get you to divulge personal information so they can steal your identity. For an unemployed person, it sounds ideal. They will try to get you to send payment for a computer and printer that you will need to use for the work. Research the company to see if they are hiring for any of the positions before agreeing to anything.

HELLO PERVERT SCAMS

This scam is when criminals email you claiming they hacked your computer and have proof you were on porn sites. They want payment, or they will send the proof to all of your contacts. They might show you pictures of your house so that you believe them.

info, often for fake travel, medical emergencies, or shipping," with operations frequently run from overseas, making them hard to prosecute.

These scams exploit respect for the military and create believable stories to justify avoiding video calls, build trust quickly, love bombing, and then ask for money, disappearing once the victim sends funds, but not always.

They use stolen photos and bios of real military personnel to create profiles on dating apps, social media such as Facebook, and other websites.

They target people who express support for the military or join related groups. Or by putting a comment on your post or on other people's comments.

They quickly profess love, marriage, and build deep emotional bonds, love bombing to create intimacy fast.

HOME ROOFING SCAMS

Common roofing scams include storm chasers who will want upfront cash, fake insurance claims, and offer free roofs. These are according to Roof Claim, Angie's List, and Universal Property. Protect yourself by verifying licenses, avoiding high-pressure, unsolicited door-to-door offers, and getting multiple written, detailed estimates. Common red flags and scams are out-of-state crews who knock on doors after severe weather, take deposits, and leave town. Contractors who claim they can cover your insurance deductible or provide a free roof, which is actually insurance fraud.

Uninvited contractors claim they found damage while working in the area. Underbidding competitors, then will charge for unexpected repairs later, that are not there.

Demanding full payment or a large cash deposit before work begins.

They use fake urgency to have you sign contracts immediately.

Ways to protect yourself verify all credentials, get at least three written estimates for the job, research the company on the BBB Better Business Bureau website, never show them your insurance policy, and do not sign immediately.

If you suspect a scam, report it to your local consumer protection office or the police.

SOLAR PANEL COMPANY SCAMS

Stay away from solar companies that claim a government program will cover the entire price of solar panels for your home. They will say they're with the government, which is a scam. If interested in getting panels, research companies and make sure they are reputable companies. If asked for advance fees to be paid or promised big savings, they are a scammer. Legitimate providers will work with you to help figure out whether solar energy is right for you. You can check the Department of the Treasury's guidance on clean energy for any answers to make your decision. Take your time and have someone look over the contract before you sign it. If they pressure you into signing, they are scammers. Pay close attention to cancellation policies, payment schedules, warranties, or if you see any hidden fees. Reputable providers will give you time to understand the contract, and make sure you sign it in writing, not electronically.

This scam is when criminals email you claiming they hacked your computer and have proof you were on porn sites. They want payment, or they will send the proof to all of your contacts. They might show you pictures of your house so that you believe them.

info, often for fake travel, medical emergencies, or shipping," with operations frequently run from overseas, making them hard to prosecute.

These scams exploit respect for the military and create believable stories to justify avoiding video calls, build trust quickly, love bombing, and then ask for money, disappearing once the victim sends funds, but not always.

They use stolen photos and bios of real military personnel to create profiles on dating apps, social media such as Facebook, and other websites.

They target people who express support for the military or join related groups. Or by putting a comment on your post or on other people's comments.

They quickly profess love, marriage, and build deep emotional bonds, love bombing to create intimacy fast.

STUDENT LOAN TEXT MESSAGE FORGIVENESS SCAMS

This text would help all who owe student loans, but it is also a scam. They want to steal your personal information. Report immediately to the FTC. If you owe the student loan, you will need to pay it. It is very, very important to be wary of all texts that do not come from a contact on your phone. Never click on any attachment or download files from a text not in your contact list. By clicking or downloading files, they can infect your phone with a virus. If you feel that the text is a scam, report it right to Apple. You can also report the message to the FTC or FCC. These agencies have been cracking down on scam text messages as well as scam calls.

SKIMMING SCAMS

$1 billion each year is what it costs financial institutions and customers due to skimming scams.

Fuel pump skimming is attached to the internal wiring of the machine, and the customer cannot see it. I usually tug on the machine to make sure nothing comes off before I insert my card. The skimmer devices store data that can be downloaded or wirelessly transferred at a later time. Choose a fuel pump that is closer to the store and where you can see the attendant best. The pumps closer to the store are least likely to be targeted by skimmers. Use a credit card as a debit card if it can be used that way, and cover the keypad when entering your PIN. It is better to enter the store and pay the attendant inside instead of paying outside at the pump. You can always tap to pay instead of inserting the card. Report skimming at ic3.gov, the FBI's Internet Crime Complaint Center (IC3).

ATM AND POS TERMINAL SKIMMING

ATM skimmer devices are inserted into the card reader within the terminal. Some skimmer devices can fit over the terminal's card reader or alongside exposed cables at a freestanding ATM located in stores. Pinhole cameras are installed around the ATM machine to record the PIN used by the customer. Keylogging pad overlays are used to get the PIN instead of cameras. It only takes seconds to install a skimming device, and the scammers have a sidekick with them to divert the attention of the attendant while they install the device. These also store data to be downloaded or transferred wirelessly at a later time to nearby devices of the scammers.

ELECTRONIC BENEFITS TRANSFER (EBT) CARD SKIMMING

Data from EBT cards have become key targets for skimming criminals. The EBT cards do not have chips, which makes it easier to compromise these cards. Criminals can cash EBT benefits at ATMs as soon as accounts receive their funding for the month. This can take place between midnight and 6:00 a.m. on the day benefits become available on the card. Also, they can cash out Supplemental Nutrition Assistance Program (SNAP) benefits between the first and tenth of the month. They will purchase bulk items such as baby formula, cooking oil, candy, and energy drinks and bars. The sad part is the money stolen cannot be reimbursed to the people it was stolen from.

HOME ADDRESS SCAM

Never give your home address to a person you do not know or have never met. While physical danger is low, they may use your address for fraudulent listings or to gain trust. If you did give the information to someone you do not know, do not panic; cease all communication immediately. Check for any unauthorized credit cards or bank activities. Monitor the mail for any signs of identity theft, like unexpected packages or bank statements. Contact local law enforcement to report any threats you may receive from the perpetrators. They can also use the address to create fake rental or product listings. Do not go to any address they give you, nor give out your home address to anyone you do not know or have ever met. For extra protection, place a fraud alert on your reports with major credit bureaus.

VANITY PUBLISHERS SCAMS

Vanity publisher scams involve companies posing as traditional publishers to charge authors high upfront fees for poor services, false promises of bestseller status, and predatory, rights-grabbing contracts.

They are called vanity presses and profit from author fees rather than book sales. Red flags include unsolicited contact, guaranteed success, and pressure to buy back your own books.

Look out for upfront fees, too-good-to-be-true offers and promises, flattery, charges to review the manuscript, hidden fees, predatory contracts, and poor-quality editing, design, and formatting for large sums of money.

Red flags include unsolicited offers, companies accepting almost any manuscript, showing they care about fees, not quality, not being able to clearly explain how they make money, and poor reputation.

Protect yourself by researching the publisher. Legitimate publishers pay *you* for rights; vanity presses make you pay *them*. Read the contract thoroughly, and consider self-publishing.

PUBLISHING COMPANY SCAMS

Archway Publishing is aware of widespread scams and misrepresentations that are targeting self-published authors. They are providing incorrect and misleading information and/or impersonating publishing companies, literary agents, editors, and other professionals in the literary industry, often using real names, trademarks, and logos to appear legitimate.

They will use the name or logo from a legitimate company. Always remember that legitimate publishers never reach out to you directly. Your literary agent is the one who submits the manuscript. A legitimate agent does not ask for money upfront. They also might tell you that the publisher is interested in publishing your book and want money from you in exchange for getting a publishing agreement for you. They also send out spam emails with links to click on. Do not click on the links, and do research to make sure all is legitimate.

A reputable literary agent will not request a fee upfront to represent a client and will not send unsolicited emails claiming to be interested in a book. If you receive an email like this, treat it with extreme caution. A legitimate agent has a website that shows what authors they represent and the books they have sold to traditional publishers.

Do not respond or engage with the email through information provided in the email. Do research on the company or individual who is offering their services to you.

Literary agents and publishers who are genuine will not communicate with potential clients through social media, personal email addresses, or phone calls. Always verify the identity of the person through public sources before engaging with the individual.

Do not provide payment information or bank information to any person or entity whose identity you have not verified. If you are unsure of the identity of the sender of a communication, do not click on any links in the email. If it sounds too good to be true, it is.

Austin Macauley Publishers (AMP) is a vanity press that operates as a pay-to-play publishing company. They are not a traditional publishing house and will try to solicit manuscripts and charge authors upfront fees. These fees can range from $3,000.00 or more. The charges are for editing, marketing, and manuscript distribution. Reviews for the company show a high risk of poor, unfulfilled promises and very little to no marketing support for authors. Due to them being a vanity press, they require contributions from authors for production costs. Traditional publishers pay authors, not ask for payment. Authors have reported being asked for thousands in contributions. Marketing, distribution, and promotion of books are not included in the fees they charge. There are also unfavorable contracts and high-volume solicitation. Be wary of publishers who request upfront payment; legitimate publishers invest in your work and do not ask for payments.

ELITE BOOKS

Elite Book Studios does not appear to be a legitimate business; it has an F rating with the BBB and numerous scam reports. Authors report paying thousands of dollars for services that were never delivered, fake royalty payments, and eventual ghosting by the company once a refund was no longer possible through credit card companies. The Better Business Bureau (BBB) shows multiple complaints from authors who believe they were scammed. The BBB has given the business an F rating. Authors reported paying for services like marketing packages, audiobook production, website bundles, and book distribution that were either poorly executed (e.g., AI-voiced audiobooks, simple PowerPoints as book trailers) or never delivered. The company's listed address appears to be fake, and lawyers hired by scammed authors have found no official record of the company. The company allegedly guarantees high returns on investments and claims ties with major retailers like Barnes & Noble, none of which appear to be true. Elite Book Studios is reported to operate with sister companies under similar names, such as Elite Book Writing, Creative Company, and Designs Company, which follow similar scam patterns. While some positive reviews exist, experts warn that many scam companies use fake testimonials and A+ ratings to appear legitimate. Reviewers report that positive reviews often appear written by the company itself. It is highly advisable to avoid doing business with Elite Book Studios and to contact your bank or credit card institution immediately to attempt to get your money back.

SIMON AND SCHUSTER PUBLISHING COMPANY

Below you will find more detailed information about how to identify these fraudulent offers and what Simon & Schuster recommends to safeguard yourself and your personal information. You may also send notices of suspected fraud to fraud@simonandschuster.com. Over the past few years, there has been a continued increase in fraudulent accounts pretending to be Simon & Schuster employees in order to trick people into applying for fake jobs, entering into bogus acquisition agreements, and sharing personal information.

Simon & Schuster does not offer jobs or publishing agreements through social media or personal email accounts. Our official company email addresses use the following domains:

- simonandschuster.com (in the USA)
- simonandschuster.com.au (in Australia)

- simonandschuster.ca (in Canada)
- simonandschuster.co.in (in India)
- simonandschuster.co.uk (in the UK)

We understand how valuable your stories are and how much time and effort you put into creating them, and the last thing we want to see is authors having their work stolen and exploited by bad actors. It has come to our attention that third parties who are unaffiliated with Simon & Schuster have been impersonating Simon & Schuster employees, literary agents, and providers of other literary services and reaching out to authors via phone calls, email, and social media, and asking them for money, manuscripts, and other personal details in exchange for assistance in having their work published. These are all scams perpetrated by nefarious third parties who have no relationship with Simon & Schuster.

In perpetuating these scams, these bad actors will sometimes create fraudulent publishing agreements (including presentation queries, endorsement letters, and pre-acquisition or pre-publishing proposals) and employment contracts using Simon & Schuster logos and marks. Although this list is not meant to be exhaustive, since these bad actors constantly assume new entity names and aliases, we have identified the following entities that have used Simon & Schuster's logos and marks without our permission in the past:

- Ace Publishing Services
- Book Solutions Press
- Brokers AB
- Independent Book Agents
- Liberal Literature
- SimonAndSchusterAcquisitions.com
- SimonAndSchusterGroup.com
- SimonAndSchusterOfficial.com
- The Literary Firm; The Literary Firm2
- ThinqPR
- Wealth Agent Network
- Writer's Torch

Here are some publishing fraud tips:

Aside from our relationship with Archway Publishing, operated by Author Solutions, Simon & Schuster is not affiliated with nor does it endorse any third-party agencies or companies that provide publishing, marketing, or any other services to authors seeking to have their work published.

Archway Publishing does not accept unsolicited manuscripts. If a third-party agency or company asks for upfront payment to help you submit your unsolicited manuscript, book trailer, or sizzle reel to Simon & Schuster, it is more than likely a scam.

We suggest that prospective authors and illustrators submit their manuscripts through a professional literary agent. We cannot recommend specific agents for your work, but the Association of American Literary Agents, Literary Marketplace, and Publishers Marketplace are good resources.

Although we do not accept any unsolicited manuscripts, in the past, we have held our BOOKS LIKE US First Novel Contest in order to facilitate accessibility to underrepresented writers and celebrate the diversity of readers across the United States. Any future iterations of the contest will be announced on our official company website, along with the contest rules and instructions on how to submit your manuscript to Simon & Schuster. Please note that we will never ask authors for payment in order to participate.

Keep in mind these common traits to help you detect a publishing scam before it's too late:

The communication, such as a phone call, social media message, or email, arrives unexpectedly.

The caller or sender asks you to provide upfront payment or banking details, claiming that you cannot proceed with your Simon & Schuster manuscript submission without these items.

The caller or sender indicates a sense of urgency, claiming that you will lose your opportunity for a Simon & Schuster book deal if you do not act immediately.

The caller or sender instructs you to never contact Simon & Schuster directly, claiming that only they have executive access or special authority to do so.

If you receive a suspicious phone call or social media message: Be cautious. As a general matter, we will not initiate contact with you via phone call, Facebook, WhatsApp, or other social media platforms.

Ask the caller or sender to email you directly from their Simon & Schuster email address. When you receive the email, pay close attention to the domain. Legitimate Simon & Schuster email addresses use the following domains: @simonandschuster.com (in the USA); @simonandschuster.ca (in Canada); @simonandschuster.com.au (in Australia); @simonandschuster.co.in (in India); and @simonandschuster.co.uk (in the UK). Do not accept indirect proof of emails from Simon & Schuster.

If you receive a suspicious email: Do not click on any links or open any attachments. Examine all aspects of the email address, word choice, tone, and formatting for mistakes or oddities. Do not reply directly. Do an online search on the exact wording of the email in case it is a previously uncovered scam and there is already a warning posted about it. Always consult with an attorney before signing any type of document, including publishing agreements. If you believe you have been the victim of a scam, we encourage you to stop communication with the bad actor, report them and/or their account to the platform you have been communicating on, contact your local law enforcement agency, and contact fraud@simonandschuster.com if you are concerned about the legitimacy of any communication purporting to be from a Simon & Schuster employee or from a third-party claiming affiliation with Simon & Schuster.

Authors should exercise caution with any unsolicited contacts who claim to be Heifetz or other known literary agents working for any book publishing agencies. Verify identities before clicking on any links by contacting the actual publishing websites, and do not submit any manuscripts unless you have a literary agent or have talked to the publishing company personally. Hachette Book Group issued an alert on its website warning all authors of scammers that are impersonating their company to get money and information. They will use the name and logo of the company, fake job interviews, and fake agents promise a fraudulent publishing contract with a large advance for Hachette and involve documents that are fraud from fake people who claim they work for Hachette. These fake employees call demanding fees before they have you sign the fake contract. More details can be read, along with tips on how to avoid publishing scams, on Hachette's website. Hachette Book Group (HBG) has advised that they have a safer effort in which they obtain manuscripts and other information from Hachette's employees, authors, and associates, and they use impersonated domain names similar to the actual company domains, using hgbusa.com rather than hbgusa.com. Check the .com address to make sure it is correct. They also use industry jargon, insider terms, and information to enhance the appearance so the emails they use look legitimate. They also claim that they found the author's work on Amazon. Red flags are also unsolicited contact, suspicious email domain (hatchettebooks.co), and vague promise of discussing publishing rights contract price upon selection.

Also be on the lookout for Harper Book Writers, which is an internationally based ghostwriting scam. These scammers target first-time authors looking for self-publication services; they offer editing, publishing, and distribution services for $4,000.00. All the services fail to deliver, and they demand thousands more for promised Barnes & Noble store placement of their book, which the store never receives, and no refund is available.

Always remember legitimate publishers do not ask for large upfront fees from their authors, nor do they promise premium bookstore placement of books for additional fees; these are all red flags. A first-time author should always research any publishing company thoroughly and ask for references from other authors they represented. Also be wary of any company that demands huge fees before providing services. A number of members have reported scam messages through contact forms on the Authors Guild member profiles or Site Builder websites. These messages are more likely fabricated by scammers and most likely generated by AI.

Red flags are generally upfront fees, unsolicited offers, guaranteed bestseller, pressure to sign, and generic praise.

Leavitt Peak Press will send out unsolicited emails saying they have discovered your old book and want to republish it at a lower price, giving the author 100 percent royalties for life. Scammers will use religious quotes and signatures that look very professional while telling you that your book has great market potential. Watch out for unrealistic royalty rates and unsolicited outreach about reprinting the book. Then they will ask for outrageous publishing and marketing fees. Leap Write Literary does the same thing as Leavitt Peak Press.

PRIMARY PUBLISHER SCAMS MIRA
(Harlequin or HarperCollins)

Harlequin and its parent company, HarperCollins, have issued many reports about impersonation scams targeting authors and job seekers. The scammers impersonate staff, editors, and literary agents to gain sensitive personal information and money. They fake acquisition offers, ask for upfront fees, phishing, and personal data, use emails that appear to come from the real companies, use poor grammar, and target both readers and reviewers via social media platforms. Protect yourself by never paying acquisition fees or manuscript submission fees. Verify email domains; they will come from @harlequin.com, @harpercollins.com, or @harpercollins.co.uk. Be wary of Gmail or other free email domains. Submit manuscripts only through the official Harlequin Submittable page (https://harlequin.submittable.com/). Do not reply or click links. Report it to fraud@harpercollins.com or Submissions@harlequin.com, and verify on LinkedIn if the person contacting you actually works for the company. Reports have indicated that Harlequin France is utilizing AI for novel translation and has terminated contracts with human translators, and an entity calling itself Harper Book Writers has been identified as a likely separate, unrelated scam operation targeting first-time authors.

AUTHORS GUILD SCAM

Authors have been warned about scammers posing as the "Authors Guild Book Acquisition Team" at "Authors Guild Literary." A complaint was filed with the World Intellectual Property Organization

(WIPO). We're thrilled to report that a WIPO arbitrator has sided with us and awarded us the fraudulent domain used in the scam, authorsguildliterary.com. The domain name will soon be transferred to our possession. We plan to post a message explaining that it was associated with fraud and that we have been awarded the domain name due to the fraud. Anyone who was scammed by "Authors Guild Literary" should report whatever information they have either to the Authors Guild or to their local attorney general's office.

NATIONAL GRID SCAM

2026 has started with National Grid warning both business and residential customers about scammers using high-pressure tactics to threaten customers with termination of service. They only do this to try to get personal information or to get you to make fraudulent payments. They will tell you that your service will be shut off within hours if you don't make the payment immediately, even if your account is up to date. Don't fall for it. Payment types they ask for are gift cards, prepaid debit cards, cryptocurrency, Venmo, or Zelle. An actual employee of the company will never ask for Social Security numbers or routing numbers of your bank over the phone to verify your identity. They also will use caller ID spoofing to show "National Grid" or, in some instances, use the company's actual toll-free customer service number. You can also ask for the last five digits of your account number to verify if they are a legitimate employee. If unsure of the call, hang up and call the official customer service number on your bill and ask questions. Report the incident to local police and the Federal Trade Commission (FTC).

DUQUESNE LIGHT SCAM

On Utility Scam Awareness Day, Duquesne Light is highlighting scam prevention to help you stop falling victim to a scam. Scams come in many forms, and all need to be vigilant to combat scammers. Calls have been received by customers from scammers telling them that a payment needs to be made immediately and their electric service will be terminated. They will ask for a prepaid type of credit card to pay off the alleged amount due. In some cases, they use spoofing phone calls to make it seem like the call is generated from Duquesne Light Company itself. A callback number will use greetings and hold messages that mimic the company. Duquesne Light will never threaten immediate shutoff for missing a payment, does not ask customers to purchase any type of prepaid cards. Never provide personal payment information if you think it is not a legitimate call, and if unsure, hang up and call 412-393-7100 to verify DLC.

JOB OPPORTUNITY AND RE-SHIPPING SCAMS

Fake job listings on LinkedIn are getting out of hand and dangerous. Victims are hired to receive, repackage, and ship stolen or counterfeit goods, not knowing they are involved in a criminal ring. Brushing packages is a scam where sellers send unsolicited, low-value items to people to post fake verified purchase reviews, boosting both the sales and ratings of the products. They use stolen or leaked personal data. The packages might contain QR codes that will lead to phishing sites to steal more information. In actuality, you are permitted to keep the items, but need to report the scam, monitor for identity theft, and should not scan the QR codes. Sellers obtain data, create fake orders, fake reviews, and fake QR codes. Remember: NEVER scan QR codes, keep items, report it, verify it is not a gift, and check for fraud.

CLICKFIX OR WINDOWE-R BROWSER SCAM

Users encounter a fake pop-up that claims to be Microsoft and says they need to fix a virus by pressing Windows Key + R, then typing a certain command into the Run box. By doing this, it installs a backdoor or malware. Any message that has you open the Run box is a major warning sign.

THE INSULIN OR MISERY SCAM

Scammers post in local city subreddits saying they need insulin in a hurry and cannot afford it, telling a fake or desperate story. When offered help, they will not meet in person and ask you to send money via CashApp or Venmo.

PACKAGE TRACKING OR DELIVERY SMISHING (SMS)

A text message claims a package (USPS, FedEx, DHL) could not be delivered due to a wrong address or unpaid customs fee, leading to a phishing website that will steal credit card details. These are often sent to all, regardless of whether they were expecting a package or not.

FACEBOOK MARKETPLACE SCAMS

Facebook Marketplace scams often involve fake sellers, stolen vehicles, or fraudulent buyers using payment apps to steal money. Red flags include high-value items listed at extremely low prices, requests for prepayments via gift cards, and pushy, urgent messages. Other marketplace scams are overpayment or fake payments, verification codes, prepayment or deposit fraud, shipping or nondelivery scams, and fake listings. Marketplace is very popular, which gives criminals access to all types of victims that rely on trust due to the Facebook brand. Always meet in person, use secure payment methods, verify profiles, and do not share personal data. If scammed, report the user to Facebook and file a complaint with the FTC at ReportFraud.ftc.gov.

FAKE PAYMENT APP REFUNDS

Scammers are able to use payment apps like Zelle or PayPal due to how popular they are. The problem is they want you to use Friends and Family options due to not being able to get a refund. They will tell you to stop payment if you used Goods and Services and switch to Friends and Family.

SMALL BUSINES INVOICE SPOOFING

Invoice spoofing is when small businesses are targeted by scammers impersonating service providers and vendors, hoping they will panic and pay invoices that are not legitimate. You need to watch for threats of termination of service, changes in payment emails, unfamiliar vendor invoices, spelling errors, or third parties asking for payments. Verify invoices by contacting the vendor, alert accounting, and report fraud to the FBI Internet Crime Complaint Center (IC3).

RECOVERY SCAMS

This is when you get scammed again. They are criminals who make it so believable that they can recoup your lost funds. They want to charge you a set fee for a nonexistent service. There are many cybersecurity services offering the same. They charge an astonishing fee and send you an email with papers that have a lot of the information blacked out and want more money to make it all visible. I did it and had to file a BBB report to find out the company was nonexistent. Now they are portraying law-assist recovery groups on social media, asking if they can help you. Please do not friend them or respond to anything from them. Another asks if you have encountered any online fraud or suffered any loss. One was portraying themselves as the actual FBI. I reported them, and they said they do not go against community rules. All are scams. Do not reply or click on any links they ask you to.

Getting scammed the first time is horrible, let alone a second time. This is what happens with recovery scams. Criminals pose as businesses who can recoup your losses from getting scammed, and they charge you a fee for these services that are nonexistent. Because many people are posting on social media platforms about being scammed, that is a place where you will find all different types of businesses claiming they can get your money back, and it never happens. You just get re-scammed again. These recovery scams lead to pig-butchering grooming scams, where criminals mainly work in groups and are based in another country. Relationships are formed by creating trust; they then snag you into cryptocurrency investments.

It is too late once you realize you got scammed; you can report it to the local authorities or a consumer advocacy group.

MONEY MULE RECRUITMENT DISGUISED AS JOBS

Criminals post fake job listings and promise you can make money quickly and work from home. The tasks for this type of work are moving money, depositing checks, and processing payments through your personal bank account. If you do not have a personal bank account, they have you open one for this job. Always protect yourself, and legitimate businesses will not ask you to transfer money to your personal accounts.

FIDDLE GAME

The fiddle game uses the drop technique. A pair of con men work together, one going into an expensive restaurant in tattered clothes, eating, and then claiming he left his wallet at home, which is nearby. The con man leaves the violin as collateral. After he leaves to retrieve his wallet, the second con man appears and offers to pay a large amount of money for the violin. The owner then comes back, having gotten the money to pay for his meal and redeem his violin. The mark, thinking he has an offer on the table from the second conspirator, then buys the violin from the player, who agrees to sell it for a certain amount that still allows the mark to make a profit from the valuable violin.

GREEN GOODS

This scam is where people are scammed into paying for counterfeit money. The victim responds to flyers circulated by the scammers, which claim to offer "genuine" counterfeit currency for sale. This currency needs to be printed with stolen engraving plates. Victims then receive offers to purchase the money at a price much less than face value. While a victim negotiates a price and is distracted, another accomplice switches the bag of money for a bag containing sawdust, green paper, or other worthless items. Victims would leave unaware of the switch and are unwilling to report the crime for fear of being arrested.

FAKE TALENT OR CASTING AGENT

In this scam, the criminals pose as a talent agent for modeling agencies in search of new talent. The model is told they will need a portfolio. The victim will pay an upfront fee to have photos taken and create their portfolio, after which they will be sent on their way in the hopes that the agent will find them work in the following weeks. Unfortunately, they never hear back from the talent agent. The fake-agent scam is often targeted at industry newcomers, since they will often lack the experience required to spot such tricks. Legitimate talent agencies advise that a genuine talent agent will never ask for money up front, as they make their entire living from commissions on their clients' earnings.

PHONY JOB OFFER SCAMS

The job scam is where a victim receives an unsolicited email claiming that they are under consideration for hiring to a new job. The email usually obtains the victim's name from social networking sites, such as LinkedIn and Monster.com. In many cases, people running these scams create fake websites listing jobs which the victim is seeking, then contact the victim to offer them one of the positions. If the victim responds to the initial email, the scammer will send additional messages to build up the victim's assurance that they are in the running, or have already been selected, for a legitimate job. This will include asking for the victim's résumé, as well as assurances that a phone interview will be the next step in the hiring process. The goal of the job-offer scam is to convince the victim to release funds or bank account information to the scammer.

FRAUDULENT DIRECTORY SOLICITATIONS

In this scam, tens of thousands of solicitations in the guise of an invoice are mailed to businesses nationwide. They contain a disclaimer such as "This is a solicitation for the order of goods or services, or both, and not a bill, invoice, or statement of account due. You are under no obligation to make any payments on account of this offer unless you accept this offer." or "THIS IS NOT A BILL. THIS IS A SOLICITATION. YOU ARE UNDER NO OBLIGATION TO PAY THE AMOUNT STATED ABOVE UNLESS YOU ACCEPT THIS OFFER." The disclaimers are designed to resemble invoices or renewals of existing advertising in a trade directory or publication. The correspondence is formatted like an invoice, often with a sequential identification number, date, personalized description of the information to be published, payment details, and total amount due, which includes a token discount if paid within a specified time period.

You can receive one like this: "Final Notice of Domain Listing" from an entity calling itself "Domain Services," which claims, "Failure to complete your domain name search engine registration by the expiration date may result in cancellation of this offer, making it difficult for your customers to locate you on the web." Public records listing legal owners of newly registered trademarks are also mined as a source of addresses for fraudulent directory solicitations. The scammers' intent is that a small percentage of businesses mistake the solicitations for invoices and pay them or mistake them for a request for corrections and updates to an existing listing. All they want is to get a businessperson's signature on the document, which serves as a pretext to bill the victim. Do not sign, and research, research, research.

JAM AUCTION

In this scam, the scammers pose as retail sales promoters. They represent a manufacturer, distributor, or set of stores. The scam requires unsuspecting victims to manage the purchases and money exchanges while the scammer maintains a high energy level. People are attracted by the crowd and will stop to gather and listen to a pitchman standing near a mass of appealing products. This scam entices victims by showing high-end products, and the scammer claims to be following rules that require him to start with smaller items. He then describes the smaller items and tells the price of the items. Many people in the crowd would like to purchase the smaller items.

You are then asked to raise your hand if you're happy with your purchase, and when hands are raised, he directs his associates to return everyone's money. This exchange is repeated with items of increasing value to establish the expectation of a pattern. Eventually, the pattern terminates by ending the "auction" without reaching the high-value items and stopping midway through a phase where the trickster retains the collected money from that round of purchases. Marks feel vaguely dissatisfied, but they have goods in their possession and the uplifting feeling of having demonstrated their own happiness several times. The marks do not realize that the total value of goods received is significantly less than the price paid in the final round. Auction or refund rounds may be interspersed with sales rounds that are not refunded.

ONLINE CAR BUYING SCAMS

You can purchase everything online, including cars, but you need to be wary of purchasing vehicles online. Ads on online auction sites, such as eBay Motors, range from inexpensive vehicles to antique vehicles. The problem is that when they list the vehicles, they take photos they find online and post them, and they actually do not own or are not in possession of said vehicles. They will have you use a well-known retailer's buyer-protection program. They also send fake invoices that look like they are from eBay Motors, asking for payment in eBay gift cards.

When you call the number on the "fake" invoice, the scammer acts like an employee of eBay Motors, building your trust. In order to find out if this is a scam, check out the seller by searching online for their name, phone number, and email address, with words such as "scam," "complaint," or "review." They will put pressure on you, won't meet in person, have an excuse for everything, want gift cards or wire transfers for payment, and also ask for shipping and transportation fees. Check the VIN of the car and get a vehicle history report. You can find information at ftc.gov/usedcars and online auction buyer resources as well. If you think it is a scam, turn it in at ftc.gov/complaint immediately.

RENTAL SCAMS

An apartment is listed for rent, often on an online forum such as Craigslist or Facebook Marketplace, at or just below market value. The seller asks for first and last month's rent upfront, sometimes also asking for references or personal information from prospective tenants. The rent payment clears the bank; the new tenants arrive with all of their possessions on moving day to find that the same unit has been rented to multiple other new tenants and that the supposed "landlord" is not the owner of the property and is nowhere to be found. This kind of scam is often performed on students planning to study abroad and seeking accommodation, as their means of checking the property are limited.

TEMU SCAM

Temu is a legitimate e-commerce platform, but it draws many scammers and impersonators, and it is a third-party marketplace model that draws more risks to people. Common scams that occur on Temu are phishing via fake affiliate links, text messages or smishing claiming shipping issues, and suspicious promotions designed to steal both financial and personal information. All users should watch for poor quality, copyright issues, and potential data-security concerns. Things to look out for are phishing and fake links, SMS/text messages, too-good-to-be-true deals, and fake accounts or customer-support impersonators. Stay safe by shopping directly on the Temu website, using secure payments, verifying communication, and researching sellers. If you feel as if you have been scammed, report it immediately to the platform and the Federal Trade Commission (FTC).

EBAY SCAMS

eBay scams target both buyers and sellers by exploiting the platform's trust and specific policy loopholes. While eBay is a legitimate marketplace, staying safe requires recognizing "off-platform" lures and shipping-related fraud. Techniques scammers use are: sellers offer a discount if you pay via Zelle, Venmo, or gift cards. These cannot be reversed, and you lose all of eBay's money-back guarantee protection. Listings for high-demand items like PS5s where the fine print reveals you are buying just the box or a digital photo; fake tracking numbers, and when you track the package, it claims it was delivered. Item is shipped to the correct address but a wrong name on the label. If you return it to the post office as not mine, eBay may view this as refused delivery; then it voids your refund rights. Top seller scams are overpayment scam, address change request, and feedback extortion.

Protect yourself by never leaving the platform, verifying emails, documenting all, and checking seller history.

AMAZON SCAMS

Amazon scams work in two ways. Scammers pretend to be Amazon representatives contacting you about a problem with your account or order. The scammers' goal is to get you to transfer money to them or to get you to give them your account logins. They also try to get you to purchase fake offers that are too hard not to purchase. This gives them the perfect opportunity to steal your credit card information. New scams are always being discovered on Amazon all the time. Common Amazon phishing scams are impersonation scams. They pretend to be an official representative of a company, government agency, or a close friend or family member. They want to gain your trust; then, once trust is gained, they will ask for money or personal information. Common scams are unauthorized purchases, where you will get a phishing email or call about an expensive purchase made on your account without your knowledge. They can use URL phishing to make you think the problem is real. Their email will contain a fake link to Amazon's website or a phone number to call regarding the purchase.

When you call or click the link, cybercriminals act like they are a representative from Amazon. The scammer will ask for your credit card details for them to stop the transaction and cancel the purchase. If you give them your information, they will then drain your bank account. Tech-support impostors call users themselves or ask the customer to contact them via a fraudulent email telling you there is a problem with your account. They urge you to install malicious apps or software to fix the issue. They can also ask you to install legitimate apps, such as AnyDesk, and ask you to give them full access, which is a scam. Scammers also pretend to be Amazon representatives and start calling, texting, and emailing Amazon Prime members, warning them about problems with their accounts. Customers are asked to pay a fake membership fee or warned that their account was accidentally charged.

This is how most scammers get you to provide your payment details, more account information, and other sensitive data. Scammers have also created fake copies of Amazon's Prime Video platform and are tricking people into giving away their login credentials. Malicious links are sent in the form of an email or an SMS message. It can look like a completely genuine message from Amazon and will prompt you to click on a link and log in to your account to solve an issue. Don't click on the link ever. Scammers trick customers. The failed delivery scam is an old online scam that targets legitimate sellers. It's pretty simple: a buyer claims that they didn't receive an order and requires a refund, while, in reality, they got it. This issue is easily resolved by using track-and-trace postage. It means that no item can be delivered without the recipient's signature.

A free gift scam comes as a message informing users that they've won a prize from Amazon but must click on a malicious link to get it delivered. The link, of course, is operated by criminals and will either inject your device with malware or steal your credentials.

Some Amazon sellers desperately want to improve listings for their products, and having tons of favorable reviews is the best way to do it. However, if the products in question are of dubious quality, these reviews are hard to get. That's where brushing scams come in, where sellers look for people's personal information, create fake orders in their name, and send their products to them.

EMAIL BANK SCAM

From mrswessingt@gmail.com

My name is Mrs. Wessing Taylor. I am the Branch Manager of the Bank where i work. There is in existence some funds that belongs to a customer who died several years back. I have contacted you because i believe you will assist me. He left an inheritance presently without any claim up till date. The said funds have been here in our Bank for many years without any claim.

Please get back to me on my direct email address, I will give you the full details of my proposal., I will await your positive response to this mail as soon as possible.

Yours sincerely
Mrs. Wessing Taylor

XFINITY EMAIL SCAM

Immediate Update Required for Account Records
abdcdshg@aol.com

MyXfinity®
Important Reminder from Comcast

Last month, we notified you about important updates to our Terms of Service, Security, and Privacy Policy. Please note that by March 13, 2025, older versions of the Comcast/Xfinity Mail system will be discontinued.

To prevent service disruption and ensure continued access to your mailbox, you must confirm your acceptance of the updated Terms of Service no later than March 13, 2025.

Re-login to update

Important: Failure to update will result in permanent loss of access to your stored data. Please do not reply to this message. This email address is not monitored, and responses will not be received.

This is a service-related email.

© 2025 Comcast. All rights reserved.

ROBINHOOD EMAIL SCAM

From: defendini_mariangela@cscsrl.it
Reply to: support@robinhood.com<207

A recent sign-in to your account was recorded from a device or network that is not typically used. The information is provided below for your reference.

Sign-in details:
Location—New Zealand
Date and time—Thursday, March 5, 2026
Device—iPhone 13 Pro Max
IP address: 60.234.77.226

If you recognize this activity, no further action is needed. If you do not recognize it or would like assistance, please contact our support team. Customer service line: +1 (888) 998-5573. Thank you. Customer support, Delilah Sims.

Remember to report the email to report-phishing@robinhood.com, and their customer service number is 1 (650) 761-7789.

No, you should not pay a traditional publisher to publish your book; they pay you and cover all costs, as their profit comes from sales, not author fees. If a company asks for money upfront to publish, it's likely a vanity press or scam, making money from you, not book sales. The exception might be certain hybrid publishers where authors share some production costs for a shared investment, but traditional routes involve no author payments.

Traditional publishing: no payment to publisher beforehand.

AMAZON EMAIL SCAM

From: Honey Dbdb
To: chgef82375wtyer@mail.
Bcc: ladyfarmer1@comcast

Thank You for Your Payment—Amazon, #237858723582375287]

BUWETUIWET823698236I...

Amazon

Thank you for your order! You have made a purchase of $618.99 from Amazon today. Details are as follows:

Order Number: #Ao_90673/56674

Date: March 2, 2026

Your order is on the way. If you need to return an item from the shipment or to manage other orders, please call us at: +1 (864) 434-8802

Product Name:

Robot Vacuum and Mop, Upgraded Bagless Robot Vacuum Cleaner with Self-Emptying Robotic Vacuum Cleaner

Qty: 2

Price: $598.99

Item subtotal (two items): $598.99

Shipping: $20.00

Total amount: $618.99

This charge will appear on your account statement as Amazon within 12 hours.

This order will be delivered today. If you haven't placed this order, then to cancel it immediately, please call: +1 (864) 434-8802

Thank you for shopping!

Please always remember to never call the numbers, reply back, click on any links, and report.

CRAIGSLIST SCAMS

There are too many scams to list, but you need to be on the lookout for all types of scams so you are not taken advantage of by anyone. Scammers list properties they don't own at low prices, asking for deposits to secure the spot before you see it.

A buyer asks for your phone number and sends a Google verification code to verify you are real; they use your phone number to set up a new account.

Fake or canceled tickets for concerts or events.

How to identify a scammer: Too good to be true; never an in-person meeting; always uses urgency and pressure; poor grammar and spelling; requests for wire transfers, prepaid cards, or apps like Western Union.

Ways to avoid scams: Always request to meet locally, cash only; never wire funds; verify items and sellers; use caution with checks; and never share codes.

If scammed, report the incident to local police, the FTC at ReportFraud.ftc.gov, and the FBI's Internet Crime Complaint Center (IC3).

CREDIT CARD SCAMS

Credit card fraud involves unauthorized use of a person's card or account information, ranging from physical theft to sophisticated digital hacking. Common examples include skimming at ATMs, phishing emails to steal credentials, card-not-present online shopping, account takeovers, and counterfeit card cloning.

Examples of credit card fraud are card skimming or shimming, card-not-present fraud, account takeover, and fake emails or texts that appear to be from legitimate companies sent to trick users into providing credit card information. Card testing is where scammers make small, cheap purchases to verify if a stolen card is active before committing a large transaction.

Use of a stolen physical card or a lost card found by a third party before it is reported.

Stealing new, inactivated credit cards directly from the mail.

Scammers retrieve card data entered on unsecured, fake, or monitored public Wi-Fi networks.

Unexpected small charges followed by large transactions.

Alerts for account changes you did not initiate. Gift card draining is very popular. Criminals steal gift cards in bulk from the racks in stores, collect the information from the cards, and return the cards to the racks in stores for people to buy. These cards are purchased and money added to them. Once money is added to the cards, the criminals will drain the money from the cards. It is safer to buy directly from the retailer's site or if cards are kept behind the counters.

CARD DECLINED SCAMS

This is a new scam where you pay for purchases online and receive a message saying your credit card was declined. They are just trying to get more pertinent information from you or have you give information for another card, and you get billed on both cards.

PAYPAL SUGAR DADDY SCAM

This is a pretty common scam where you get contacted through a social media app where you have a profile picture. The "sugar daddy" is an older male who contacts you, saying they have lots of money and are looking for companionship. They tell you they will send you money on PayPal or other online cash payment apps. They will send you a screenshot of a "pending transaction," which is fake, and ask you to send them a smaller amount. Please do not fall for it.

PAYPAL SCAMS

I had a scary thing happen last night! Just as I was going to bed, I got a series of emails from PayPal regarding a new PayPal account. Someone tried to set up a new account using the email address that I set up specifically for tour guiding. They used a different name, phone number, and SSN, but my email. Luckily, I caught it before I clicked on "verify your email." I checked the return email, and they were all valid emails from PayPal. I tried logging into that account by trying to change the password, but that's when I noticed the erroneous number, and it told me my SSN was wrong.

PayPal scams involve phishing emails, fake invoices, and social engineering that is specifically designed to steal money or account credentials by creating a false sense of urgency. Scammers will also use overpayment schemes, phishing links that direct users to fake login pages, friends and family so you can't be refunded anything, will cancel payment if you use goods and services, shipping address changes, and advance fee fraud. You can protect yourself by never calling numbers you receive in a suspicious email, verifying transactions directly on the official PayPal app, and reporting phishing to phishing@paypal.com. Keep safe by checking to make sure the email is @paypal.com, log into the site directly, verify payment, ignore urgent demands, and report suspicious activity.

CASHAPP SCAMS

Cash App is right alongside the major digital wallets in the marketplace today, but it is more than just a digital wallet. Cash App works like Venmo, and it goes beyond payments. Cash App offers options to invest in stocks, buy and sell Bitcoin, free tax filing, and it is a savings account as well. You can connect a debit card to the app also. Cash App is a financial platform and not a bank. Funds kept in it are not protected by the Federal Deposit Insurance Corporation (FDIC), but you can protect your funds by keeping a Cash App debit card or through a sponsored account. A sponsored account is an account for a child aged thirteen to seventeen, legally owned by an adult.

More than a quarter million dollars move through the app, and most definitely scammers work their way into the mix. From fake customer support scams and fraudulent payment requests to phishing links and money-flipping, scammers use all methods to steal money and personal information from victims. Money-flipping scams are all over social media, and scammers promise big returns on money that victims put down through secret methods that guarantee results. Scams start out slowly as the scammer builds trust with the victim. Money results start from $10.00 to $50.00 that the scammer invests.

Days later, the scammer sends the victim a real return, which might be two times or four times the original amount. This might go on awhile before they up the payment to hundreds or thousands of dollars. Then, the scammer disappears, never to be heard from again. Deposit scams can occur if someone is looking for a pet, apartment, or used car online. Scammers take advantage of that with Cash App as well. This scam riffs on phony classified listings, and items are held for the victim until they can make a full payment or sign the lease; then they find out there is no pet, car, or apartment, and the money and scammer are long gone.

Accidental payment scams are when scammers flood a long list of Cash App users with messages telling them they sent money to the victim by error and want it returned immediately, in hope of having the victim return the money. Only send money to friends and family, block strangers who ask for money, lock your app with your fingerprint, face, or PIN; better yet, close and delete the app. If you did send money by error, you can return it to the same sender. Never send money from your personal accounts, never share your app's login or password credentials, and if you suspect fraud, report it to Cash App.

VENMO SCAMS

Venmo scams involve hackers impersonating support, accidental payments, and fraudulent buyers using stolen funds, leading to irreversible losses. They use phishing, fake invoices, and urgent fake account-suspension messages to steal credentials. Send money only to people you know and never click on any links. Look out for accidental transfer scams, fake customer support or phishing emails, overpayment or fake buyer scams, fake prizes or giveaways, romance or family impersonation, and fake job or deposit scams. Protect yourself by enabling multifactor authentication (MFA), verifying recipients, never giving away codes, using official channels and privacy settings, and reporting fraud email to phishing@venmo.com.

ZELLE SCAMS

Zelle is a peer-to-peer transfer service that enables people to send and receive money via an app by using a phone number, username, or email. It's a convenient way to send money because it's fast and free. Sending money to other people has never been easier, whether paying for goods and services or sending money to someone for a special occasion. Zelle can transfer your money in minutes. However, these platforms also give way to fraud and theft. With Zelle scams on the rise, keeping your finances safe is more important than ever. Keep reading to hear from experts about how to spot fraud and tips to protect your money.

Zelle scammers trick users into sending money through fake alerts, impostor calls, or fake sales. Scammers ask you to do a reverse fake charge by sending money to yourself or a "secure" account. The Zelle network connects more than 2,200 bank and credit union brands of all sizes, enabling consumers and businesses to send digital payments to people and businesses they know and trust with an eligible bank account.

Money is available directly in bank accounts within minutes when the recipient is already enrolled with Zelle. Zelle account takeovers happen when scammers hack your Zelle or bank account. They usually change your password and lock you out to transfer the money to themselves. Scammers need login information to access your account, which they can obtain through fraudulent emails, texts, or calls posing as your bank.

If you've had the same password for the past year or tend to keep your login details somewhere that's easily accessible, it's easy to fall for an impersonation scam because scammers pretend to be someone you know. They may pose as a family member, romantic interest, or financial institution, hoping to catch you in a vulnerable moment so they can request funds. Fake invoice Zelle scams are when fraudulent activity regarding pay statements or invoices occurs via email.

Victims are prompted to click a link to go directly to the app, but instead, the malicious link downloads malware onto the person's phone or computer. The scammer can then gain access to your personal information from the victim's device. To avoid this type of scam, consider adding extra security software to your phone or computer. Fake invoices or pay statements are sent via email.

One example is an email saying that someone has deposited money in their Zelle account. They want you to click a link that states it will take you to the original app, but the link downloads malware onto your electronic device. The scammer can then gain personal information from the victim's device. To avoid this type of scam, consider adding extra security software to your phone or computer. The scammers also target unsuspecting buyers who send money through the peer-to-peer app to purchase an item from a seller they connected with online. The seller suggests to the buyer, "Zelle me." The buyer sends the money, and the item is never received, and the seller disappears.

How to avoid Zelle scams is to keep your finances safe, especially when sending money or making a purchase. Easy ways to protect yourself are to know Zelle's rules, verify identity, send only to people you know, beware of pressure or urgency to pay, never share codes, use two-step verification, send a small test payment, and report it to the Federal Trade Commission (FTC) website.

WHATS APP, TELEGRAM, TEAMS, AND FACEBOOK SCAM

Telegram and WhatsApp scammers will steal a well-known person's identity and start a chat with you if you comment on their fake page elsewhere. They will get to know you there, then, after they know you are comfortable talking to them, they will ask if you have Telegram or WhatsApp to move the conversation to. They will tell you it is safer. They will also ask you to get in touch with their management team to pay for a meet-and-greet or pay a membership fee. No true celebrity will ask for your money. Their management team will not ask for money, nor do they have Gmail email accounts. Beware!

These platforms are unsupervised and harder to report problems on the apps. Try to check to see if the user is legitimate. Do not send photos or personal information, and never give them money, which they will try to extract from you with a sad story. You can try to block, report, and delete, but it won't help. Social media scams are on the rise more and more each day. More than $2.7 billion has been lost to victims falling prey mainly to romance scams on all social media platforms. $943 million was lost on social media platforms for romance scams and was reported to the FBI Internet Crime Complaint Center (IC3).

On social media platforms, there are also investment and online shopping scams that target unsuspecting and lonely older victims. The scammers are so good at what they do and use fake profiles, hacked accounts, and phishing links to target users on platforms like Facebook and Instagram. A wannabe fake person friends you on a social media app and then tells you to move to a social media platform that their team recommended. They keep getting into my Facebook account, and now they want money so they can monitor my accounts from scammers. Red flags do not speak grammatically correctly.

In the video warnings, he states, "I only have one social media platform, and me and my team do not reach out nor ask for money for anything. I am not in financial trouble, sick, running from the law. Please report and block." They can send an AI voicemail, which you can tell is altered. This is what the altered message said: "Don't expect me to show you my personal details. I've told you to save your money, so I still am confused as to why you don't want to let everything be."

Teams scams involve cybercriminals impersonating IT support, executives, or colleagues to steal credentials, install malware, or solicit funds. Techniques scammers use are fake, urgent tech support, phishing messages with malicious links, and external user impersonation. Protect yourself by verifying unexpected requests, never downloading software from unknown users, and reporting suspicious activity.

Scammers use Teams chats, sometimes with a fake check mark emoji, and use their profile name to appear as a trusted colleague, celebrity, or supervisor. They send malicious links or ask you to email or text their manager for a fee to meet them in person, want photos of you, and upload files containing malware. Protect yourself by verifying the identity of anyone asking for urgent actions such as passwords, never clicking on links or giving them access to your electronic device, using built-in reporting tools like the Phish Alarm button to report suspicious, unsolicited messages, and enabling multifactor authentication.

If you believe you have been targeted, report the incident immediately. Major warning signs to look out for are urgent requests for money, too-good-to-be-true offers, and pressure to move conversations to apps like WhatsApp, Signal, Teams, and Telegram. All social media platforms are breeding places to be scammed.

Please stay away from them all for your own safety. Cease all communication with all you are talking to and report them all. They will sell your contact information, and they will never stop bothering you. You will get scammers from all over asking for money, phones, gift cards, addresses, and login information.

DO NOT GIVE ANY PERSONAL INFORMATION OUT TO ANYONE, NEVER EVER!

Do not send to friends and family; always send money under goods and services. Scammers will message from unknown numbers claiming a new number and asking for urgent financial help. They claim they sent you a six-digit code by error and ask for the code, job and investment scams, fake support and security, screen-mirroring QR codes, and lottery gift card scams. Never share codes, verify identities, enable two-step verification, and report and block.

WHISPR SCAMS

Whispr is a new social app designed for anonymous chatting. It allows users to send and receive messages, photos, and videos without revealing their identity. While it may seem like a fun way to communicate, it's important to understand the potential risks, especially for kids.

Whispr is about anonymity, where users can chat with others without revealing their identity; secret conversations, where chats are private without any personal information attached to them; and shared content, such as photos, anonymous messages, and videos. The dangers are that anonymity makes it easier for users to be cruel, spreading hate or bullying without consequences, which can be cyberbullying; talking to people you don't know, putting them at risk of online predators; the sharing of explicit or harmful material, which may be difficult to trace; and anonymity, which can lead to risky behaviors or conversations that may negatively affect your child's emotional well-being.

How to protect all is to limit who can message or view your child's activity, keep track of all interactions and conversations, explain why anonymous chats can be risky and encourage them to talk to you about anything uncomfortable. Whispr doesn't have built-in parental controls, so be proactive by talking to your child about safe app use, and let them know they can come to you if they experience bullying, inappropriate content, or anything that feels off.

Explain why anonymous chats can be risky and encourage them to talk to you about anything uncomfortable. Whispr doesn't have built-in parental controls, so be proactive by talking to your child about safe app use, and tell them that they can come to you if they experience bullying, inappropriate content, or anything that feels off. It's very important to keep an eye on your kids if they are using this app. Stay informed, set boundaries, and keep the conversation going about online safety.

LET'S SWITCH TO A SAFER CHAT

"Let's switch to a safer chat" is how the scammers start to gain your trust, and they use your emotions to do this. It doesn't start with money for a while, and then the urgency starts and the "love bomb." They will send morning love notes telling you how much you mean to them, along with an endearment that they will call you. They are good at remembering details, tell you they can't call or video chat with you. It is against management rules. They respond to a comment you made on a fake profile of a person whose identity they stole. It is usually a well-known celebrity. They use this person's identity to take money from you. Pressure and urgency come next, then you doubt me and don't trust me.

When they ask to move again and send a link to click on, be wary. It comes up malicious link.

I stared at the link again. It was trying so hard to look like a real chat service. The name was close enough to feel familiar. The design was clean. The continue button looked exactly like the kind you'd tap without thinking. Dangerous site blocked.

You can go to the chat and ask why they sent the malicious link.

Why can't we just talk here, and they tell you their account is being monitored. They then say trust me and send another link. They weren't moving you for convenience, but were moving you to a place where it is easier to manipulate. Never click on the link. You finally realize they are after your trust. The scam isn't always about sending me $500. Sometimes it's just a link, little detour, new chat, verification, private photo, voice note. Romance scams start with greed, lonely people, a sob story, wire transfer. The next ones start with familiarity, words that make you lower your guard, my love, baby, I feel safe with you, and can we talk privately? They don't need your password. They just need one moment where your heart overrides your brain. The one thing that can save you is when it stops being chat link and becomes log in here, verify your phone, confirm your identity, help me with something, I'm stuck. Scammers don't start with threats; they start with trust.

LATEST CELEBRITY SCAMS

All celebrity scams start with a message that resembles something you think is from your favorite actor. The message could be from Brad Pitt, George Clooney, Keanu Reeves, Jennifer Aniston, Martin Henderson, or many more. All claim that they liked a comment you made on their page or they liked your profile on Instagram. You are flattered and think you are chatting with the celebrity themselves. In actuality, the message is not from the celebrity, but from a scammer. It starts with a message from someone who looks just like your favorite actor. Maybe Brad Pitt, George Clooney, or even Keanu Reeves. They say they've seen your Instagram profile, admire your smile, or appreciate your kindness. You're flattered because you think you are chatting with the actual celebrity. The message is from a scammer with a fake profile and stolen pictures that are AI-generated. They prey on your emotions to gain your trust. After trust is there, they ask for help using urgency for legal matters.

Celebrity romance scams are the cruelest and most dangerous scams. One woman lost $15,000.00 to a scammer claiming to be George Clooney. The scammers use both AI-generated voice messages and videos. Over a 2.5-year period, a Florida woman sold her car, took out a home equity loan, and had her bank account used to launder money. She thought she was helping Keanu Reeves and did all of that, which had her lose close to $160,000.00.

Recently, Reese Witherspoon posted an Instagram story and TikTok video warning fans about scammers posing as her on both of those platforms, contacting unwary fans who think they are having a real relationship with her that just leads to their being scammed. Despite efforts of Instagram and TikTok to take down phony Reese Witherspoon accounts, there are presently dozens of such accounts, including @reesewitherspoon private. Making the problem worse, these phony accounts will actually post actual videos of Reese Witherspoon to make the accounts appear legitimate and make fans who are likely to engage when they are contacted through the account by the scammer posing as Witherspoon.

Confirm on the celebrity's website to see if they really do endorse a particular product. As for celebrity-based romance scams, it is important to recognize that celebrities aren't reaching out online to people they have never met to start romantic relationships. Any DM you get from a celebrity asking for money, donations, help with a private matter, inviting you to join a secret fan club, or do anything with cryptocurrencies is a scam. Any message that indicates they need help with a legal issue, are stuck while traveling, want to reward you if you cover a small fee, or need gift cards is also a scam.

Most commonly used tactics scammers use are urgency and don't tell anyone we are talking.

Signs to look out for are they contact you using a private message and start a romance immediately, avoid real-time video calls and use scripts, keep the relationship a secret, assets are frozen, ask for wire transfer, crypto, gift cards, and pressure you, they claim you do not trust them.

No real-life celebrity will message or ask for money, never send money, don't share personal information, and don't feel pressured to help someone you don't know.

Country singer Cooper Alan is the victim of widespread impersonation by scammers using fake social media accounts, TikTok, Facebook, Instagram, to scam fans. The scammers use Telegram or WhatsApp, request money, gift cards, or personal information, sometimes using AI-generated voice notes.

AARP THE PERFECT SCAM

AARP's weekly podcast, *The Perfect ScamSM*, tells the stories of people who discover they were a target of a scam. Bob Sullivan, the host of the podcast, introduces listeners to victims who experienced scams, as well as leading experts who pull back the curtain on how scammers operate.

INSIDE A GOLD COIN SCAM STING

A Florida man, who was targeted by a PayPal impostor scam, helped police with a sting operation.

Brian discovers he was likely the target of a PayPal impostor scam, which involved crypto kiosks and gold exchanges. He worked with police detectives to set up a sting operation to catch the scammers.

When Brian received emails from PayPal, he thought it was the refund he'd been waiting for, but instead he was drawn into a scam that had him running all over town feeding money into crypto kiosks and exchanging cash for gold coins to hand off to a courier. Brian soon grows suspicious, but resists the urge to confront the scammers and went directly to the police. Brian helped detectives in setting up a sting operation to catch the courier and expose a crime ring.

$1 MILLION THEFT: TECH SCAM LEAVES TEACHER SHAKEN

Occupied with serious health and family issues, Joyce was targeted in a tech scam that drained her of her retirement funds.

Joyce is a retired teacher who works part-time with special needs kids. She was recently divorced, facing a health issue, and is the primary caregiver for her 96-year-old mother. With all of this weighing on her, she becomes the target of a tech support scam. By scaring her, the scammers stole over $1 million from her!

Help Us Slam the Scam!

Learn about common tactics and how to recognize the signs. Signs to look for are unexpected problems or offers of prizes or government benefit increase.

Pressure to act immediately, request for unusual payments like cryptocurrency, gift cards, gold bars, cash, or wire transfers, even with the promise of keeping your money safe.

To protect yourself, spread the word and report suspicious activity.

COOPER ALAN SCAM

Scammers are posing as Cooper Alan to steal money from fans, with reports of fans losing thousands of dollars. They contact you through social media and then move to WhatsApp or Telegram to solicit money, gift cards, or, in one reported case, $5,000.

Cooper Alan publicly has stated he does not reach out to people directly, will never ask for money, and that any such interaction is a scam. These scammers report hundreds of fake accounts per week. If someone claims to be Cooper Alan, do not send money, report the account immediately, and block it.

BLAKE SHELTON SCAM AND ROBERT PLANT FROM LED ZEPPELIN

A woman in her 60s entered a contest for a $1 million prize and to be chosen for Blake Shelton's fan of the year. To enter this contest, you had to wire a total of $17,500.00. It was a scam.

It was not Blake Shelton's manager who was communicating to the woman, it was a scammer.

Scammers who pose as the celebrities follow a playbook and nurture the victim before they ask for money. It turns out to be a romance scam. The scammers invent excuses why they need the money. Another woman reported sending Robert Plant from the group Led Zeppelin $23,000.00.

SANDRA BULLOCK AND JENNIFER ANISTON SCAM

A man from Michigan lost $3,000.00 that he put on Apple gift cards to his new love interest, a scammer, who claimed to be Jennifer Aniston. He did file a report with the Better Business Bureau's Scam Tracker.

Next, "Sandra Bullock" was chatting on Telegram, which is a breeding ground for scammers. The scammer claimed she loved the person and wanted to be with them. The victim lost $2,100.00.

HELEN MIRREN SCAM

People have been using my name to front a false charity, which is sending out messages offering a large sum of money and asking people to respond to helenmirencharity@gmail.com. She says that is not her email address nor her. This is a scam, and the original messages are coming from drogogo91@gmail.com and refer to it as a genuine charity.

SCAM NEWS ON KEITH URBAN.

Based on recent reports, Keith Urban has been heavily targeted by impersonation scams, particularly following his divorce in late 2025–26. Scammers are exploiting the news to create fake, emotional, and financial scenarios to target fans, especially on social media platforms like Facebook and Instagram.

LATEST NEWS AND TACTICS INVOLVING URBAN.

"Secret Relationship" Romance Scams
Impersonating Family Members

Fake "Exclusive Content and Information"
Fundraising (Private Meeting Scams)
Fake "Social Media Profiles"
Ways to Stay Safe:

Keith Urban and his team will never message you directly to ask for money, gift cards, or personal information.

Verify profiles. Official accounts like Facebook and Instagram have a blue verification checkmark, but remember these can also be fake.

Report and block. If you receive messages from a "Keith Urban" account asking for money, report it to the platform immediately.

Never click links. Never click links in suspicious messages promising private, exclusive content or, in this case, leaked information about his private life.

ROMANCE SCAMS

These scams will never go away, and more and more identity theft of famous people is happening every day. These people who steal a person's identity are known as catfishers. They find a victim and get to know them intimately. They find you when you comment on a fake profile on social media. They reel you in with all the right questions, and then they drop the "love bomb" on you. Then watch out. Now they ask for your financial help. They find out your likes and dislikes by what you post about on social media, so do not comment frequently. Stay on the platform; don't let them isolate you on another app; they want you to trust only them. They tend to start love bombing within a week, always starting with "hey your profile caught my eye" or "hey beautiful/handsome." The scammers always use terms like dear, my love, babe, baby, my queen. Regularly say they are widowed with a kid; a significant other cheated or had an accident or cancer. They mostly say they are God-fearing and want a partner who is God-fearing. They rarely read replies that are "off script," just ignoring what you've said and still coming with the questions. Most answers that aren't simple will be copy-and-paste paragraphs (they stand out a mile), and they ALWAYS ask, "have you eaten?" It's a thing that Nigerians say daily.

Their grammar is poor: that's instead of that, common instead of come on, "can we get to know ourselves better" is another favorite. They will also always try to move your chat to somewhere like Google Chat, WhatsApp, Telegram, or Signal, because these are harder to trace. The gaslighting is next level; the manipulation will only confuse you, so be aware. Some of them are good, like really good. Their English is on point for days; then all of a sudden, you'll get a sentence or a message that just doesn't come across the way it should, based on where they say they are from or what job they claim to do. It's usually the US military, talking about fighting Taliban in Syria, or engineers on oil rigs, doctors working for the UN on some far-flung continent, and they ALWAYS say that they can't call or video call due to operational security. Remember to be aware that they want gift cards (iTunes, Google Play Store, Steam cards, Amazon gift cards), cryptocurrency, or Cash App payments. All of these are sold within their network. Broken phones or having to pay for data are another couple of go-to excuses, as well as sending you their belongings, which come with a hefty customs bill, or receiving paperwork on their behalf, which is just an attempt to get your address. They are demanding and always wanting to know where you are, asking for pictures as proof of things they want to know or asking you to do so, so please never divulge real information to anyone you meet online, because it will be passed on to others in their network or sold on the dark web. These are all red-flag points to look out for. I've been scammed, and it was horrendous when I realized, so if this paragraph can make someone stop and think, stop and reverse image search, even then it's worthwhile.

ROMANCE SCAMS ON PLATFORMS 2026

Romance scams are becoming more frequent, and with AI technology becoming increasingly more sophisticated, these traps are hurting more and more people.

In 2026, romance scams remain a significant concern, leveraging advanced technology like AI deepfakes and sophisticated psychological tactics such as "Business Proposal Trap" to defraud victims on social media, dating apps, and professional networking platforms. Do not listen to any sad sob stories, nor the "I love you" shortly after you start talking; do not let them isolate you by moving from platform to platform. They do not want you telling anyone you are talking to them.

Never send any funds to anyone that you do not know or have never met in person. They will send you social media pictures of them. Do a reverse image search to check the picture. They send AI video chats by depicting the voice of the person they are impersonating, so insist on a video call.

They will tell you their bank account is frozen when they start to ask for money. Keep all correspondence from where you are talking. Most importantly, REPORT!

NIGERIAN ROMANCE SCAMMERS

This is where the total of romance scams starts. They are like a sweatshop but use computers and have scripts they follow when taking advantage of unsuspecting victims. They tell you what you want to hear, then tell you they love you to get funds from you. Most of them steal identities from famous celebrities whom they know people follow and watch what the victims comment on. The unsuspecting people who get scammed and the people they are impersonating are the victims and always realize they were not at fault; the scammers are the ones at fault! These Nigerian men are good at what they do and defraud many millions of dollars. Beware!

ROMANCE MILITARY SCAMS GLOBAL

Global military romance scams involve "fraudsters using fake online profiles with stolen photos of real service members to build emotional relationships, leveraging military service as a cover for deployment, urgent needs, or inability to meet, then manipulating victims into sending money, gift cards, or personal info, often for fake travel, medical emergencies, or shipping," with operations frequently run from overseas, making them hard to prosecute.

These scams exploit respect for the military and create believable stories to justify avoiding video calls, build trust quickly, love-bomb, and then ask for money, disappearing once the victim sends funds, but not always.

They use stolen photos and bios of real military personnel to create profiles on dating apps, social media such as Facebook, and other websites.

They target people who express support for the military or join related groups, or by putting a comment on your post or on other people's comments.

They quickly profess love, marriage, and build deep emotional bonds, love-bombing to create intimacy fast.

They claim to be deployed overseas in the Middle East, on peacekeeping missions, to justify not meeting or video calling due to security or poor internet.

Once they establish your trust, they invent emergencies, medical bills, travel home, shipping vehicles, or needing funds for gift cards or wire transfers.

The scammers often work in groups, sharing scripts, and may involve fake intermediaries for payments.

They request money or gift cards, especially for emergencies or travel. They use very affectionate language very early in the relationship. They will not do video chat or meet in person due to deployment issues.

The stories they tell you do not add up or involve high-ranking officers needing permission for things.

Be wary of anyone met online who quickly professes love and asks for money. Never send money or share personal info with someone you haven't met in person. Be suspicious if they can't video call or meet. Report fake profiles to the dating site or other media platforms and authorities like the Federal Trade Commission (FTC) Internet Crime Complaint Center (IC3).

Scammers create fake profiles, often stealing photos and celebrities' identities from military personnel and celebrity pages to build fake relationships and always plead for money using different tactics. Scammers mimic friends, family, or celebrities to request money or promote fraudulent deals. They say their bank account is frozen, have health issues, need a new phone, need help with internet payments, have court fines that need to be paid, and whatever ploy they can use to prey on your emotions. Some of the scammers also find a victim through dating apps, or the victims make a remark on fake celebrities' social media pages. Social media is a breeding place for celebrity romance scams. They move you from one platform to another to keep you isolated and want you to not tell anyone you are talking to them. A romance scam is set apart from other scams due to the scammer gaining your trust and then dropping the "love bomb." They communicate with you many times over a span of weeks and months, gaining your trust. They then tell you that their account is frozen and they cannot gain access to the account and need help financially. They say they need the funds now and give you tons of options to help send them money.

According to the Federal Trade Commission (FTC), $2.95 billion has been reported as a loss each year from victims who got scammed by wannabe actors and actresses who stole the identities of these celebrities. Nearly 60,000 people over the age of fifty have reported being scammed and lost all of their savings. Celebrity management often charges for official meet-and-greets, but it includes concert tickets, VIP packages, or conventions. The fees can range from hundreds to thousands of dollars, though legitimate management never asks for money via private messages, social media, or to claim prizes, which are scams. These are found on official ticketing sites, nowhere else. Never buy a fan card or membership cards to meet a celebrity or send money to someone in a private chat telling you they are a celebrity's manager.

No real celebrity will ever ask fans to pay for a fan card, membership card, or VIP card to communicate with them, meet them, or receive special treatment. Any request for money, crypto, or gift cards is a scam. They want to establish a relationship as quickly as possible, endear themselves to the victim, and gain trust. Scammers may propose marriage and make plans to meet in person, but that will never happen. Eventually, they will ask for money. They are experts at what they do and will seem genuine, caring, and believable. The sad part is that when you cease all communication, you feel as if you lost your best friend because of the connection you have had with them. It is a devastating feeling to go through.

Red flags to look out for are a wrong-number text, they want to talk to you directly, they live far away, they are constantly in contact, make plans, but something always arises, need money for an emergency, have an investment opportunity, ask you to donate to their charity, vanish, and always come back. Protect yourself by not sharing personal information or pictures, blocking all communication, talking to someone about it, doing reverse imaging, not sending money, reporting the scammer to the FBI's Internet Crime Complaint Center (IC3.gov), joining a peer group, and telling your story to all.

One celebrity in particular whose identity was stolen makes appeals all the time, saying they or their management will not reach out to you, they are not on social media, if you are talking to someone on social media platforms, cease all communication, and they nor their management will ask for any money. Multiple romance scams have been reported involving individuals impersonating New Zealand actor Martin Henderson, best known for his role in the Netflix series Virgin River. These scammers use fake social media profiles and, in some cases, AI-generated voice messages to deceive victims into believing they are in a relationship with the actor.

In early 2025, one woman in particular was scammed over a two-year period by a scammer posing as a wannabe Martin Henderson. The scammer told her lies of corrupt bosses, frozen accounts, and an escape from Hollywood, while constantly requesting financial support.

Over time, Lea transferred enormous sums to support her fictional fiancé's supposed troubles, including $30,000 for a private jet that was allegedly canceled when he was "jailed" for breaking his contract, $10,000 for bail money, $12,000 in gift cards, $56,000 in shipping fees for a nonexistent box containing valuables, and multiple Bitcoin transfers totaling over $375,000.

Eventually, her bank flagged her transactions as potential money laundering and closed her account of eighteen years.

The scammer contacted the victim on a Virgin River fan page, claimed to be the actor's agent, and then posed as Henderson, communicating via WeChat and Telegram. Her world came crashing down when a friend sent her a news article showing the real Martin Henderson participating in a bike rally in New Zealand, at the same time he was supposedly hospitalized in South Africa. The woman said, "My head is all over the place, and I felt very foolish having opened my heart," and "I was severely manipulated during some very traumatic events in my life." Her scam followed a pattern seen in many high-profile romance fraud cases, including a similar scam with the celebrity Brad Pitt, who scammed a victim out of $1.5 million. They all use AI-generated voice messages to mimic Henderson's voice and provided elaborate, fake stories about being in jail or having health crises to solicit money. The victim was then convinced to move to New Zealand in December 2024, only to realize the deception in February 2025 when the real Henderson was spotted at a public event, contradicting the scammer's story that he was in a hospital in South Africa. The sad part is more and more women from around the world have come forward, reporting losses of tens of thousands of dollars to similar scams.

Martin Henderson's Response

Martin Henderson has publicly addressed these scams, calling them "sad and horrific." An official warning by the actor himself states through his official Instagram that he does not engage in private chats, does not DM fans, and never asks for money or gift cards. He also expressed concern that AI and "deepfake" technologies make it easier for scammers to impersonate him and has numerously warned fans to be skeptical, ignore any requests for money, and only follow his verified social media accounts.

Romance scams can do much damage to you; they cause both financial and emotional pain. She is now struggling to come to terms with the emotional betrayal. "The loss of money is painful, but the loss of what I thought was a real relationship is even worse," she told reporters at the NZ Herald. Lea's story echoes that of Ayleen Charlotte, a victim of the infamous Tinder Swindler. In our recent interview with Ayleen, she shared how romance scams leave victims not only financially ruined but emotionally shattered as well. The psychological trauma can take years to overcome, with victims struggling to rebuild their trust in relationships and financial security.

Ayleen emphasized that scammers use charm and persuasion to exploit deep-seated human desires for connection and love. She also highlighted the importance of raising awareness and empowering victims to speak out without shame.

Warning signs are a false sense of urgency to make you act quickly, asking for payment via wire transfers, gift cards, or cryptocurrency, or too-good-to-be-true deals.

To protect yourself against romance scams, they warn you against trusting online relationships that move quickly or involve requests for money; no celebrity or legitimate romantic interest will ask for money, Bitcoin, or gift cards; verify identities; report fraud to platforms such as Instagram and law enforcement, and to the FBI's IC3. Protect yourself also by verifying identities, limiting who can see your posts and personal information, not sending photos or personal information, using strong, unique passwords and enabling 2FA, and not clicking on unsolicited links or engaging with unknown profiles.

You can specifically secure your Instagram account against these threats: go to settings, security, two-step-factor authentication to set up SMS or an authentication app.

Another romance scam is the oil rig scam. The scammer claims to be working overseas and uses fake oil rig scammer pictures of males or well-known male oil rig scammer names to build their credibility. They send pictures to the unsuspecting victim and claim that is them in the picture. Verify the image and research any suspicious claims they make. They usually start out on a dating app or social media app like Threads. They prey on your emotions to gain your trust. One rule of thumb for meeting people online is to be leery of them. They will tell you that they can't use video chat, can't meet in person, or just about any excuse they can give you to keep you talking to them. They reel you in like a fish on a hook.

Romance scammers are great manipulators and love to steal people's images to scam online. There are a few male oil rig workers that scammers like to use in their scams. They photoshop the image and send it to convince the victim they are actually on an oil rig. They then make up a wonderful story about a part breaking on the rig and money is needed to get the part, which is not cheap. They even send a photo of the so-called oil rig engineer to manipulate you in many ways to get you to send them money. Red flags to look out for are love bombing, guilt trips, gaslighting, where they have you questioning your own reality, blame-shifting, periods of neglect, asking for small requests at first, building trust over time, and wanting you to say yes. Do not send any personal information to them. Protect yourself by verifying image authenticity, consulting with friends, seeking professional advice, filing all necessary reports, and most importantly, learning to say no.

VIRGIN RIVER SCAMS

There has been a surge in romance scams targeting fans of the Netflix series Virgin River, with major incidents involving an impostor of star Martin Henderson, who plays Jack Sheridan, defrauding a victim of over $375,000. These scams often use AI-assisted voice cloning and fake, private, or fan-run social media accounts to manipulate victims.

A major "Virgin River" scam involved an American woman ("Lea") who was defrauded of over $375,000 over two years starting in early 2023 by someone posing as Martin Henderson on WhatsApp and Telegram.

The scammer used AI-generated voice messages to sound like Henderson, claiming to be in love, wanting to leave the acting world, and planning a life together.

The victim was convinced to pay for a private jet, "bail" money, gift cards, Bitcoin, and twenty-five MacBooks, often with the excuse that the actor's funds were frozen.

The interaction began on a Virgin River fan Facebook page, where the scammer initially posed as the actor.

The victim moved to New Zealand to meet the impostor before discovering the fraud when a friend showed her an article proving the real Martin Henderson was elsewhere.

Martin Henderson has stated on Instagram that he does not have any other accounts and never messages fans privately.

The real actor nor his management team will ever ask fans for money, gift cards, or financial assistance.

Scammers avoid video calls or use poor-quality video or voice, sometimes with AI, to mimic actors.

Official cast members do not use platforms like WhatsApp, Telegram, or Zangi for fan interaction.

Fans are urged to report any fake profiles to the social media platform immediately.

Martin Henderson and his co-star, Alexandra Breckenridge, have both warned fans about these ongoing scams.

Stay safe by only trusting verified, blue-check accounts on Instagram.

Report fraudulent profiles to the platforms Facebook and Instagram and block them immediately.

Assume anyone messaging you claiming to be a celebrity is a scammer.

Note: There are also separate scams targeting Internet users that use the name "Virgin" (such as "Virgin Media" scams), but the above information specifically relates to the "Virgin River" show/actor scams.

EMAIL SCAMS FROM SOCIAL SECURITY

Dino
lowejerax191@gmail.com
My email address
Social Security Office of the Inspector General
Notification
February 16, 2026
SSA-OIG-0226-C
Official notice no. 6,886,825

This notification is to let you know that your Social Security number (SSN) record has been temporarily flagged for administrative review following an internal examination.

Why did you get this?

A technical inconsistency pertaining to your earnings verification was discovered during our regular OIG examination. To finish the evaluation and prevent an administrative hold-up.

To speed up processing, please mention case number OIG-A279 when you call. You will be walked through the verification process by our representatives, which usually takes three to five minutes.

VALENTINE'S DAY SCAMS

Scammers are set to target those looking for love with romance scams. Now, with the development of AI and the potential for deepfakes, the romance scammer playbook has just become much more convincing and is ready to prey on those on the dating scene in 2026.

In an effort to warn people against handing over money to what seems to be a secret admirer, the Joint Policing Cybercrime

Coordination Centre (JPC3) has released a guide to spotting these scams before they take hold.

According to the JPC3, romance scams were the third-most-reported type of scam in Australia in 2025, with 3,432 incidents, as per Scamwatch. This represented a $28 million loss for victims, with a dramatic percentage of those scams being reported following online contact.

A request or pressure to move a conversation off a dating or social media platform not long after initial contact can be a first red flag.

The reason being that dating and social media platforms often have safety features and detection measures, which scammers want to get away from as soon as possible.

Once a scammer has moved the conversation to a different platform, the victim is also isolated, meaning it can be easier to prey on their vulnerability, optimism, and emotional investment to stop them walking away. Other warning signs include lots of attention or affection, such as love-bombing, oversharing of personal or emotional stories, having reasons why they can't meet in person or video chat, and encouraging victims to keep their interactions private from family and friends. These scammers, particularly those that work in overseas call centers, have standardized playbooks designed to maximize success. This means scammers are often speaking to multiple victims at a time, with the intention of getting them on the hook and then continuing to scam them over a long period of time and generate a continuous flow of cash.

Scammers who mostly work in call centers or boiler rooms overseas have scripts and playbooks to follow, receive coaching, and operate 24/7 to deploy the best tactics to deceive innocent victims.

Their main agenda is to hook victims quickly, but they are then in it for the long haul, looking to draw the connection out for as long as possible to scam as much money as they can.

This creates a double hit for their victims, who, when the truth eventually emerges, are left to grieve not only the emotional impact of a relationship they believed was real but also the financial damage, shame, isolation, and loss of trust.

Romance scams can look similar to the following: you receive an unsolicited message from a stranger that may or may not appear to be legitimate. They show interest in you and try to gain your interest, often by stating they have similar or identical interests. They push to move the conversation to another platform, using excuses like giving you their number to push the conversation to text or saying that the platform you are currently on is one they don't use often or is difficult to use. This may seem like a progression of the relationship, but it's a way to keep the victim isolated and vulnerable. At this stage, the scammer begins to slowly develop more of a relationship, bringing walls down until they find a suitable way to begin persuading the victim to hand over money.

Protect yourself by verifying as much as you can. This means reverse image searching, checking social media, and more. Ask for an in-person meeting or video call, but beware of AI-generated video calls. These can be identified with visual or audio glitches, signs of AI generation such as a robotic voice, unrealistic answers and changes in appearance, or low-quality footage, which may be used to hide these artifacts. If you're doubtful, speak to friends and family for their opinions. Most importantly, don't send money until you can be 100 percent sure the person is legitimate, and outside of this, make sure their intentions are real. Even if the person is real, they still might try to get money out of you.

AI SCAMS

AI is a term for technology applications that perform tasks typically associated with human intelligence, such as learning, reasoning, problem-solving, perception, and decision-making. Some examples of AI include, but are not limited to, autocorrect on your computer or phone, voice typing, customer service chatbots, facial recognition software, photo and video editors, language translators, and more.

Scammers use AI to clone a person's voice, often using just a three-second audio sample from social media, to impersonate loved ones or authority figures. A common, urgent emergency call might involve a child or grandchild claiming to be in jail or injured to get immediate money. The scammers can create realistic yet fake videos or images. They are used for pretending to be a company CEO in a fake video conference to trick employees to transfer funds, sending altered images to family members, claiming to have kidnapped a loved one. AI is used to build perfect profiles and engage in long-term grooming to win trust before soliciting money, sometimes called pig butchering. AI helps to generate grammatically correct, highly personalized, and convincing phishing emails that easily bypass spam filters. Scammers use AI to build fake, convincing websites that promise high-return, low-risk cryptocurrency opportunities, or they post fake jobs to collect personal information. Malicious actors inject fake customer support numbers into search results, such as Google AI Overviews, that are then presented as fact to users.

Things to look out for is a sense of panic designed to force quick decisions without thinking, such as immediate requests for money. Requests for payment in cryptocurrency, gift cards, or wire transfers. In deepfake videos, look for unnatural blinking, jerky movements, or strange lighting. In audio, listen for a robotic tone or unusual pauses. Unexpected contact, even if it appears to come from a trusted source.

Ways to protect yourself are to create secret words or phrases with family and friends to verify their identity during an unexpected, urgent call. If a loved one calls for help, hang up and call them back on their known, direct number, not the one that called you. A scammer relies on panic. Take your time to pause, think, and verify. Enable a two-factor login on all sensitive accounts to prevent hackers from taking over, even if they have your password. Be wary of too-good-to-be-true offers. If you suspect an AI scam, report it to the Federal Trade Commission (FTC) at ReportFraud.ftc.gov. Many legitimate companies use Artificial Intelligence (AI) to help us in our daily lives. Unfortunately, because AI is a relatively new and developing technology, scammers are also increasingly using these tools to harm and deceive. Follow these tips to help recognize the red flags of AI scams and better protect your money.

Scammers may use AI to closely mimic human behavior, such as language use or cultural traits, to add credibility to their scams.

It can sometimes be hard to tell what is real and what is not. Some common types of AI scams include: scammers use AI to compile images from many databases to create fake photos or videos that look and sound real. These scams may use images of someone you know or a well-known celebrity or public figure to add credibility to their messages.

If you think you have been a victim of an AI scam, or suspect one, submit a complaint or call (866) 275-2677 for assistance. Dfpi.ca.gov

We strongly recommend that you DO NOT reply to or click on anything sent to you by a fraudulent account, but DO report them to the platform where they contacted you.

As of late 2025 and early 2026, the US Department of Veterans Affairs (VA) has issued urgent warnings regarding several active scams and hoaxes targeting veterans, their families, and survivors. These scams frequently involve impersonating VA officials to steal money or sensitive personal information.

Reference
Veterans Benefits Administration (.gov)

A top scam are fake letters, emails, or texts pretending to be from the VA, claiming the veteran was overpaid benefits and now owes money. The scammer uses fake logos and fraudulent, high-pressure tactics to demand immediate repayment via gift cards, wire transfers, or cryptocurrency. Non-legitimate companies are targeting veterans by charging illegal fees to help file initial claims or promising to maximize disability ratings. They may pressure veterans to sign contracts that take a percentage of their benefits, pension poaching, false claims stating that the VA is issuing special life insurance dividends to veterans, and romance and friendship scams. Protect yourself by verifying on VA.gov or call 1-800-827-1000. Never pay for help. The VA does not call, text, or email to demand payment by gift cards or cryptocurrency, and use the VA Office of General Counsel Accreditation Search Tool to verify if a representative is authorized to help.

If you have been targeted by a scam, report the fraud by contacting the VA at:

1-800-827-1000 or report it to the VA Office of Inspector General (OIG). Report scams to vsafe.gov or call 1-833-38VSAFE (1-833-388-7233), and report the fraud to the Federal Trade Commission at ReportFraud.ftc.gov.

All scammers are clever and are targeting veterans, their surviving spouses, and family members who receive VA benefits. They pretend to be official VA representatives and use official communication channels to demand repayment for alleged benefits overpayments. Fraudulent letters, emails, and texts often include fake VA letterheads and logos, making it difficult to distinguish genuine VA communications from scams.

Tactics that are used by scammers are fake VA letterheads and logos, and even spoofed phone numbers to make their communication appear authentic. They also claim you have been overpaid on your VA benefits and now owe money back to the VA. They use pressure tactics to have you make immediate payments directly to them instead of through official VA payment channels. Payments they ask for are wire transfers, bitcoin, prepaid debit cards, money transfers, or gift cards. They also ask for sensitive information, such as your VA login credentials, password, or financial information.

If you receive a letter or any communication about a VA benefits overpayment, log into your official VA.gov account for verification to see if you truly owe money. The VA website will provide clear information on whether you owe any money. If you do owe money, the VA's Debt Management Center (DMC) offers many repayment options.

Never share login information: VA will never ask for your login credentials or passwords.

Be cautious of unsolicited contact: Be wary of unsolicited emails or texts asking for personal details or directing you to external websites that are not part of VA.gov.

Do not pay upfront fees: If someone demands an upfront payment to help with your VA debt or claims. You can find a VA-accredited representative to assist you at www.va.gov/get-help-from-accredited-representative/find-rep.

Avoid clicking on unknown or suspicious messages: Be cautious if you receive an email or text asking for your personal information. Scammers often create fake links or attachments to trick you into downloading malware or malicious code to steal your data. Always review the sender's information carefully and avoid clicking on links or attachments from unknown sources.

Never share sensitive information: Secure personally identifying information (PII) and financial information. Never share sensitive information, such as social security numbers, bank account details, or credit card information when responding to unsolicited requests.

Being aware of common scam tactics and following recommended precautions can significantly reduce your risk of falling victim to fraud. Always verify information through VA.gov and treat any suspicious communication with caution. Protecting your personal information and promptly reporting any suspicious activity can help ensure your benefits and personal data remain protected. The VA offers a wide range of tools and resources to combat fraud and protect veterans' benefits. To learn more, please visit the VBA fraud prevention page. Stay safe and vigilant! Contact the VA: If you have been the target of a scam or suspect fraudulent activity, contact the VA immediately at 1-800-827-1000.

File a complaint: You can also report fraud to the Federal Trade Commission (FTC).

Veterans who suspect they have experienced fraud can find out more and report to the appropriate agency online at VSAFE.gov or by calling (833) 38V-SAFE.

VA LIFE INSURANCE DIVIDEND SCAM

There is no truth that a special dividend for veterans who do or don't have government life insurance has been passed by Congress. Veterans receive emails or written correspondence announcing that Congress has passed a law that would pay a dividend of several hundred dollars to veterans who had been or are currently enrolled in SGLI plans. This is a scam! Do not open the file or divulge any personal information to that fraudulent email.

The only dividends ever paid by VA are on active government life insurance policies. Dividends on active policies have been paid annually for many years, and policyholders do not need to apply for them. These special dividend rumors are spread by well-meaning people who want to help veterans but fail to check out their sources before passing the information along to others. Here is an example of a notice seen in veterans' magazines, union newspapers, fraternal publications, newspapers, and every other publication imaginable. This scam has appeared in many forms and seems to change to fit the times and started in the 1960s as a rumor about veterans with WWII insurance. It has been adapted to state that a dividend is being paid on Servicemembers' Group Life Insurance (SGLI) or Veterans' Group Life Insurance (VGLI) coverage. VA has done everything possible to stop this rumor, but it still continues no matter what they try.

You can help by returning the false information you received to its source and telling whoever gave it to you that you know for certain there is no such dividend. If you have any questions about this hoax, or any other matter related to veterans' issues, please don't hesitate to contact the VA organization.

Sample fraud notice.

> To all Veterans and Families of Veterans
>
> If you are a Veteran, or if any of your relatives fall under that category, you may be interested in the following information. A bill was recently passed by Congress entitling Veterans to a dividend on the GI Insurance they had while in the service. Both current and former military personnel are entitled to this dividend regardless. If you are a Veteran, or if any of your relatives fall under that category, you may be interested in the of whether or not they still carry the insurance. If you are eligible, you WILL NOT receive the

dividend unless YOU ASK for it! The Veterans Administration will review each individual case and determine eligibility. A general schedule of dividends earned is as follows:

2 YEARS OF SERVICE: $261.00
3 YEARS OF SERVICE: $391.04
4 YEARS OF SERVICE: $528.00

To apply for the dividend, write to the VETERANS CENTER, P.O. BOX 8079, PHILADELPHIA, PA 19101. REMEMBER: THE VETERANS ADMINISTRATION WILL NOT AUTOMATICALLY SEND YOU THE DIVIDEND. YOU MUST APPLY FOR IT. Complete the form below.

In accordance with the bill recently passed by Congress, I am applying for the "SGLI" insurance dividend based on my prior military service. The specifies of my service are as follows:

NAME: ______________________
ADDRESS: ______________________
DATE OF ENTRY INTO ACTIVE SERVICE: ______

DATE OF DISCHARGE: ______________
SGLI NO. (If Known): ______________
BRANCH OF SERVICE: ______________
SERVICE NUMBER: ______________
DATE OF BIRTH: ______________

FBI WARNS OF IMPERSONATION SCAMS

The FBI and the AARP Fraud Watch Network Hotline (877-908-3360) are warning people that fake agent scams, where impostors pose as government officials, are on the rise.

The criminals impersonate a wide range of local, state, and federal government agencies, and, along with the use of artificial intelligence, make these scams harder than ever to detect.

How this scam works is you will receive a call, text, or email from someone claiming to be from the FBI or another government agency. They could tell you that a warrant for your arrest has been issued. Or they will tell you that your identity was stolen and used to buy child pornography or to launder money. They use urgency for your help to catch the criminals who stole your identity and ask you to transfer your money to them for safekeeping. They will ask you to not tell anyone what is going on, and it must be kept quiet.

You should know what they tell you does sound professional, but it is a scam. They spoof legitimate phone numbers and include personal details as well. Real names of FBI agents or local officials are used to make it appear they are legitimate if you search online for them. Their aim is to steal both personal information and money from you. Always remember that government officials never contact you out of the blue to get any forms of payment from you or ask you to wire money, send cryptocurrency, gold, or gift cards.

You should not communicate with anyone who contacts you claiming to be a local, state, or federal agent. Contact the agency to verify the telephone number or official website. Never share personal information, and if you feel it is a scam, go to IdentityTheft.gov for step-by-step directions on protecting yourself or recovery from identity fraud.

US MARSHALS SERVICE

You receive a phone call or text message where federal agents are being impersonated by someone trying to get money. They tell you that you will be arrested and legal action taken against you if you do not pay. They also claim contempt of court for failing to comply by not paying an unpaid fine or missing jury duty. Fake warrants, court orders, or subpoenas are sent with forged signatures from federal judges. Caller ID is spoofed to make it look like calls are originally from the local courthouse or a government agency. They ask for untraceable payment methods, which are hard to trace, like Bitcoin, cryptocurrency, gift cards, or wire transfers. Always remember federal agents never contact you on the phone nor text you.

SCAMS IN PENNSYLVANIA

Scams in Pennsylvania are on the rise. In 2035, over $75 million was lost due to AI-enhanced fraud targeting seniors and residents. Top threats include fake jobs, smishing fake PA Turnpike texts, government impostor or warrant scams, and rental fraud. Protect yourself by never paying via gift cards or cryptocurrency and verifying with agencies directly.

Pennsylvania task job scams are when victims are promised high pay for simple online tasks, which can be liking videos or rating items, only to have their savings stolen, with reported losses up to $220,000.

PA Turnpike smishing is a fake text message SMS phishing claiming you owe outstanding tolls and asks you to click a link to a fraudulent site.

Government impostor warrant scams are when scammers claim to be the police or the sheriff. They say that you have a warrant or missed jury duty and want immediate payment to avoid being arrested.

Fraudulent ads on social media offer cheap rentals, requiring upfront payments for fake applications, often targeting those looking for housing.

Fraudulent donors send fake checks to organizations for too much money, then request a partial refund before the check bounces.

Thieves in parking lots, such as Giant Eagle, use skimmers or apps to steal credit card data while appearing to take donations.

Protect yourself by verifying information, never pay to get paid, and avoid paying with gift cards, cryptocurrency, or wire transfers, check Turnpike accounts only on official channels using the official PA Turnpike E-ZPass website or the PA Toll Pay app, and contact the PA Office of Attorney General's Bureau of Consumer Protection or the local police.

LOCAL PENNSYLVANIA POLICE SCAMS

The scams are hitting locally in Pennsylvania. The Crafton Borough Police Department posted on Facebook that they have been seeing an increase in a new fake landlord scam, which has been targeting people who are looking for housing to rent. They warned that all who are seeking housing or looking to rent should be wary of impostors who are posing as landlords of properties that might actually be listed legitimately or not. Never send money through any online apps without first meeting the actual person and verifying that they are the real owners of the property that they are advertising and that you are interested in. You should be able to have access to the property and be able to see the place, both inside and outside.

The police have recently been made aware of scammers posing as the landlord of a certain property. The scammer asked that money be sent to them through PayPal.

A legitimate landlord would never have any issues verifying who they are, showing the property, and verifying their information before asking for any payments. Any pressure or quick requests for money being sent without first meeting and verifying this information will lead to a loss of your money from a scam like this.

If you are involved in a scam like this, contact police immediately. Property owners should take necessary precautions and ensure potential customers have specific information on hand.

INDIANA PENNSYLVANIA REAL ESTATE SCAMS

More than $2 million in Indiana County properties are the target of the new out-of-state scheme.

The Indiana County Recorder of Deeds office has had to void at least ten faulty deeds since November. It just gets worse, and every instance needs to be on the lookout at all times.

Several residents in northern Indiana County called the recorder's office last summer after unknown vehicles were spotted driving around, going down roads of vacant property of their neighbors, writing down mailbox numbers. They also tried to question the scammers and saw Texas license plates. They'd claim that they were with the gas or electric company.

In November, something didn't look quite right on a deed for a $450,000 property.

All three brothers' signatures looked authentic, along with the notary's signature as well. A gentleman in northern Indiana County allegedly gave his property to his three sons, who live out of state, and was not sure if this was a legitimate land transfer. Not long after the deed transfer was submitted, the recorder's office got a call from the owner saying the property was not put up for sale by the family. Two weeks later, after that deed, two more miles away, the scammers tried to commit the same process again. The recorder's office immediately knew what was taking place.

The purchase of that property was canceled, and fortunately no money was lost.

The scammers wrote fake deeds and contacted local realtors to try and sell properties that never belonged to them.

They claim they have a medical emergency in Texas and need to hurry up and sell the property. They are in a hurry and have a medical emergency. They're trying to get owners who have property here but live in another state.

These faulty deeds are being seen more and more and happening over and over. The I's are not dotted, and the T's are not crossed, and that is how they end up calling the courthouse.

If one of the fake deeds is accepted by an agent, the scammers are trying to get on Zoom calls with realtors to get more information.

There have been multiple calls to many different agents in both Indiana and in Blairsville County. One of our agents took them up on the call. They were able to, and I don't know how, get into his bank accounts. He was able to work with his bank to get the money back.

Workers at the recorder's office have also heard about scammers calling people and pretending to be them.

Constantly, the scammers are asking elderly people to sell their property. They'll say they don't want to sell. Why are you calling me?

The scammers take it one step further and go to a realtor and say that they're that person and show a fake ID for that person. Now, the realtors are checking IDs, and they're forging IDs.

There have been at least ten instances like this in the county. None of them has been approved. State police are actively investigating.

Local realtors and county workers are on high alert, and they want the public to be the same way.

They've never seen anything like this. It's really scary. If you're an absentee owner and you are not around here, make some phone calls and do some checking in.

If they're calling and harassing you on the phone, just hang up on them or don't talk to them. Other county recorders are not going through what is happening in other counties in Pennsylvania. You have to go local. Even in the Pittsburgh communities, you have to go with your local attorneys and realtors to sell your property.

The county has a property alert system that you can sign up for to get alerts about activity involving a property that belongs to you.

CREDIT CARD SCAM AT LOCAL GROCERY STORE PARKING LOT

Shaler police have started an investigation after they say four men solicited donations at a Giant Eagle parking lot. It is believed those involved are part of an out-of-state theft ring.

The incident occurred outside of the store on Butler Plank Road on Monday. Lt. Watkins of the Shaler Police Department spoke with a local Pittsburgh news station. The individuals were asking for donations. They claimed a relative of theirs had passed away, and they needed to raise funds for a funeral.

The scammers intimidated the victims by surrounding them as they were by their cars.

Instead of accepting cash donations, the scammers were asking for credit card information. They had a hand-held scanning device to scan the card numbers.

The victims that had used their credit card to make a donation of 20 or 30 dollars later found out that they were charged up to $3,000 instead of the 20 or 30 dollars.

It was noted the scammers appeared to be part of an out-of-state theft ring, and out-of-state police where the incident took place are working with local, state, and federal authorities to investigate the scale of the operation.

Police are urging the public to be cautious when donating and to be aware of suspicious activities.

Cash is king. Pretty much every organization will take cash payments, so when people are looking to get your credit card information, that is a red flag.

The Mt. Lebanon Police Department and other regional law enforcement agencies are receiving increasing reports of scams about naked picture blackmail targeting juveniles. Scammers befriend and message juveniles on social media platforms such as Instagram, Snapchat, Roblox, Discord, and others. Scammers pretend to be a member of the opposite sex, similar in age to the victim, and develop a relationship over days or weeks. They convince the victim to send naked photos of themselves through the platform or as text messages. Scammers often use photos of prior victims to make the exchange seem mutual. The scammers then use the photos to blackmail the victims, demanding money. Although this scam also has targeted adults, there has been an increase in juvenile victims.

MAILBOX THEFTS

Residents in Western Pennsylvania, including Mt. Lebanon, have been victims of theft after their mail has been stolen from United States Postal Service mailboxes. Sensitive personal information sent through the mail can be used to steal your identity and result in fraudulent accounts opened in your name. Thieves are also filing fraudulent tax returns and cashing fraudulent checks.

To ensure your personal information is not compromised, the Mt. Lebanon Police Department recommends you use online bill pay where possible. If you must mail a check or paperwork that has your debit or credit card information written on it, we recommend you mail it inside a local post office, as opposed to using an outdoor mailbox of any kind.

PAY NOW SCAMS

Never will a legitimate biller, utility, or nonprofit organization ask you to pay for service or an overdue fee with gift cards or bitcoin.

If a caller asks you to download an app on your phone or computer, do not do it. Never withdraw large sums of money for a caller for them to pick up at your home.

The IRS will never call you on the phone, and they do *not* take gift cards or bitcoin, and they do not make house calls.

These are all parts of recent scams.

FAILURE TO APPEAR AT COURT OR DOCTORS OFFICE

Scammers say they are local police officers or a Physician's Assistant calling from a doctor's office. They say you were to appear at court for a hearing or missed a doctor's appointment. The scammers tell you that if you do not pay cash as a civil fine for missing the hearing or doctor's appointment, you can go to jail. The phone number which they call from is altered to appear to be from the Pittsburgh Police Dept. Zone 1, and they inform the victim to take the cash to the parking lot of the Pittsburgh Police Dept. Zone 1 building.

This is a scam, and the Pittsburgh Police Dept. has been notified. If you receive a phone call like this, please hang up the phone and do not provide any information. If you have any additional questions, please call 911 and request a phone call from the Mt. Lebanon Police Department.

Mtlebanon.org

Pittsburgh Police has learned that numerous residents have received phone calls where the caller claims to be a lieutenant with the Bureau.

The person informs them that they have an outstanding warrant and documents to serve. They then ask for money in order to have the warrant cleared. THIS IS A SCAM.

Pittsburgh Police will never serve documents over the phone or ask for money at any time.

A money mule scam is a type of money laundering operation in which criminals recruit individuals (mules) to receive and transfer illegally acquired money on their behalf. The funds often come from online scams like romance cons, fraudulent job offers, and investment schemes.

MONEY MULE SCAMS

A money mule is someone who transfers or moves illegally acquired money on behalf of someone else. Criminals recruit money mules to help launder their money.

Scammers use various tactics to trick people into becoming money mules. The general process involves scammers reaching out through unsolicited emails, social media messages, online dating apps, or fake job advertisements promising easy money for minimal effort. The scammer spends time building a trusting relationship in a romance scam or a seemingly legitimate employer-employee relationship in a job scam.

The mule is asked to use their personal bank account to receive funds obtained through illegal activities. Once the money is in their account, they are instructed to quickly withdraw it or transfer it elsewhere, often via wire transfer, gift cards, or cryptocurrency, keeping a small commission for themselves.

The initial deposit will eventually bounce or be identified as fraudulent. When law enforcement traces the illegal funds, they lead back to the money mule's account, while the actual criminals disappear.

Warning signs to look out for are unsolicited job offers or online messages promising a significant amount of money for little work.

The job description is vague, and the employer only communicates through web-based email like Gmail or Yahoo or messaging apps.

You are asked to use your personal bank account to move company funds.

An online acquaintance or romantic partner whom you have not met in person requests to use your bank account for receiving or forwarding money.

You are told to keep a portion of the transferred funds as payment.

A sense of urgency or pressure to act quickly, preventing you from thinking critically or researching the offer.

Becoming a money mule is illegal, even if you are unaware of the underlying crime. Consequences can include prosecution for crimes such as money laundering, wire fraud, or bank fraud, which can lead to fines and imprisonment. Being held personally liable for repaying the stolen money to the bank or other victims.

Damage to your personal finances, credit history, and potential identity theft.

If you suspect you're involved in a money mule scam, stop all communication with the individuals involved. Freeze or close the account and prevent further activity. Report the crime to law enforcement, such as the FBI's Internet Crime Complaint Center (IC3) and the Federal Trade Commission (FTC). Keep records of all correspondence and transactions as evidence.

FRAUD RECOVERY SCAMS

Fraud recovery scams or refund scams target previous scam victims by falsely promising to recover lost funds for an upfront fee. Often perpetrated by the original scammers, these frauds use fake identities such as government agents or lawyers in order to steal more money and personal information. Never pay upfront fees to recover lost money, as legitimate law enforcement does not charge for these services.

A stranger contacts you about a previous scam, demands payment before any money is recovered, poses as the FTC, FBI, police, or attorneys, requests payment in cryptocurrency, gift cards, or wire transfers, and promises that your money is guaranteed to be returned.

Steps to protect yourself: Do not respond to calls or emails promising to recover lost funds. If someone claims to be from a government agency, look up their official contact information independently. Never provide bank account numbers, SSNs, or other personal details to unsolicited callers.

POLICE SCAMS

The St. Clair Township Police Department and East Liverpool Police Department have just been notified that there are scammers attempting to collect money from residents, indicating that they are associated with our department, and the number that they are using is connected to our dispatch center. We can assure you that we would never solicit money via phone and ask you for any personal information and/or credit card information. Please be cautious.

PA ATTORNEY GENERAL SCAM

Pennsylvania residents should know that government agencies do not conduct official business through unsolicited text messages, and most do not communicate by email unless the recipient has specifically requested email correspondence.

Attorney General Dave Sunday is warning Pennsylvanians about a text message and email scam in which individuals receive fraudulent messages claiming to be from a municipal court, alleging an unpaid parking ticket that requires immediate payment or a court appearance. Another message sent via text or email alleges the recipient has an unpaid parking ticket that requires immediate payment or an appearance in court. A scare tactic they use is that if you don't pay, the message says you could be hit with additional fines, have your driver's license suspended, or face other consequences.

Many of the scam messages appear to come from the Philadelphia Municipal Court but can also appear to come from other courts or government agencies.

The message can include a link to make a payment. If you think that you've been a target of this scam, do not click the link or copy it into another web browser.

Scammers rely on fear, urgency, and embarrassment to pressure people into acting quickly. Before responding to any messages of any kind, take a moment to verify their legitimacy. If you're unsure, do not click any links. Ask a trusted loved one for help or contact my office to report the potential scam.

Government agencies don't use unsolicited texts for official business, according to the attorney general's office, and most don't communicate through email unless specifically directed.

Anyone who has received one of these scam messages is urged to file a complaint with the Office of Attorney General's Bureau of Consumer Protection. A copy of the text or email should be included in the complaint. Any unsolicited or suspicious text messages or emails should be reported as spam or junk through your phone or email provider. Consumers can also block the number or email address.

Anyone who has received one of these scam messages should file a complaint and include a copy of the email or text message received to the Office of Attorney General's Bureau of Consumer Protection online, by phone at 1-800-441-2555, or by emailing scams@attorneygeneral.gov.

Yes, it is generally recommended to keep the app, along with all associated evidence, immediately after being scammed, but with specifics regarding security. Documentation, such as chat logs, transaction histories, usernames, and screenshots, is very crucial for law enforcement, bank disputes, and investigations.

Here is a breakdown of why you should keep the app and evidence and how to handle it safely: banks and payment platforms require detailed proof of fraud to initiate chargebacks or reverse transactions.

Police and agencies like the FTC or IC3 need records, usernames, phone numbers, and email addresses to build a case and hopefully recover funds. Keeping the app allows you to document the full scope of the scam, including fake support accounts or related fraudulent profiles. Reporting details helps authorities map out the scammers' network.

While you should keep the evidence, you must protect yourself from further harm. Take screenshots of the scammer's profile, conversation history, and payment details. Do not send any more money. Block and report the scammer. Change passwords if the app used is a banking or payment app such as Cash App or PayPal. Enable two-factor authentication and check for unauthorized linked devices. If deceived into downloading a malicious app or an APK file, delete it immediately after taking a screenshot of its icon, as these can contain keyloggers.

Remove the app immediately after documenting it to stop scammers from stealing more data.

Once all evidence has been given to the authorities and your bank, and you have secured your accounts, you can remove the app.

Remember, deleting the app does not close your account or stop recurring charges. You must follow the platform's formal account-closure process.

COMMON ONLINE COLLEGE EDUCATION SCAMS

Online education scams have ghost students using stolen identities to steal financial aid, fake diploma mills, and phishing for student loan information. These scammers will promise you fast degrees, require upfront fees, or pressure victims into immediate payment to avoid losing accredited status. Ghost student fraud entails scammers using your stolen personal information such as SSNs and your name to enable them to enroll in community colleges, apply for financial aid, and pocket the funds, leaving victims with debt and damaged credit.

Diploma mills or fake accreditation organizations offer degrees for money without legitimate coursework, examinations, or instructor interaction.

Scholarship and financial aid scammers claim to have guaranteed scholarships, or they say they are from the government or loan servicers demanding immediate payment for debt relief.

Fake online courses and platforms are non-existent schools or courses with no educational value, and they operate as a front for collecting personal information and astronomical fees.

Book and material scams offer low-cost textbooks that you pay for and never receive. They want to get your credit card information.

How to avoid and identify accreditation scams is to check for legitimate accreditation agencies. Legitimate institutions do not guarantee high-paying jobs or degrees with little effort. Be wary of pressure tactics requiring immediate tuition or processing fee payments. Never share your FSA ID username and password with anyone. Look for detailed syllabi, qualified instructors, and verified reviews of the institution.

If you suspect a scam, you should report it to the Federal Trade Commission, the Department of Education, or your local law enforcement.

BRICK AND MORTAR COLLEGE SCAMS

College scams commonly target students and parents through fake scholarship offers, tuition payment fraud, and housing scams to steal money or identities. Ghost student scams have seen criminals use AI and stolen identities to enroll in community colleges, stealing millions in financial aid.

Common, dangerous college-related scams are scholarship and grant scams, where scammers trick you into paying fees for scholarship databases that require upfront fees. Ghost student fraud entails using identity theft to enroll in online community college courses, and they will siphon financial aid.

You may receive phishing emails or calls claiming unpaid tuition to extort immediate payment, or fake rental listings that require a deposit before seeing a property.

Companies also promise to lower or forgive your student loans for a fee. The US Department of Education never charges to manage loans.

Too-good-to-be-true job postings on LinkedIn or email are designed to steal personal information or collect upfront fees for supplies.

Protect yourself by never paying for scholarships or financial aid. Handle tuition, aid, or job offers directly through official school channels or employers, never through unsolicited links or numbers, and never share SSNs or bank details with unknown parties. Check your credit report regularly to ensure no fraudulent, unauthorized enrollment has occurred in your name.

Unfortunately, not all offers to help pay down student loans are altruistic. The Federal Trade Commission (FTC) recently announced that it shut down a scam that stole student loan borrowers out of $23 million.

According to reports, the scammers lured their victims using false promises to pay down student loan debt and lower monthly payments. All the while, the thieves were diverting payments to their own accounts, and in some cases, they had even changed the borrower's contact information on US Department of Education websites in order to limit the victim's contact with the legitimate federal loan servicers. Some borrowers didn't realize for years that their student loans weren't being repaid.

Protect yourself by visiting the US Department of Education website at studentaid.gov/repay if you have federal student loans. If you have private loans, speak directly with your loan servicer. For more information, visit ftc.gov/studentloans.

Scammers know that students may be searching for apartments, books, and moving services. They also know that they may be able to lure students with a great deal, ask for payment upfront, and then simply never deliver the promised goods or services.

Protect yourself by avoiding making online purchases without validating the website and checking online reviews. See if the company is listed with the Better Business Bureau (BBB). Make sure they have a real physical address and phone number, and get a referral from family or friends. Never rent an apartment without seeing it inside and outside. Do not make payments over the phone.

College students can log a lot of time on public Wi-Fi networks.

Scammers exploit security flaws on a public Wi-Fi router. When a user logs on to a banking website or shops online while on a public network, personal or financial information entered can be at risk of exposure. Avoid logging into banking apps while on public Wi-Fi networks, and don't visit any website on public Wi-Fi that requires you to enter your password.

Scammers may be lurking on social media platforms, even on pages that seem to belong to legitimate organizations.

ANTIVIRUS SCAMS

Anti-virus scams use fake, high-pressure pop-ups, emails, or browser alerts to claim your computer is infected, forcing you to pay for useless software or grant remote access to criminals. Legitimate security alerts do not demand immediate payment, provide phone numbers for support, or lock your browser.

Messages appearing in your browser that look like system alerts, often with loud noises, flashing, or countdown timers, claiming your computer is 100% infected.

Scammers pose as reputable companies like Norton or McAfee through email or phone, claiming your subscription has expired or a virus was found, to steal credit card details or install malware.

A pop-up that locks your browser, making it impossible to close without calling a support number.

Emails with fake invoices for antivirus renewals to trick you into calling a number or clicking malicious links.

Protect yourself by not panicking, ignoring cold calls, never calling the number listed in a suspicious pop-up, only downloading software directly from vendor websites like Norton, McAfee, or Bitdefender, and, if worried, running a scan using your actual, reputable antivirus software.

If you have already paid or given remote access, contact your bank immediately and run a full malware scan.

OFFICIAL WINNING NOTIFICATION

Hi Roberta, 7245619714

My name is Linda Grizzle. My son and I were recently blessed to win $167.3 million. As part of our personal mission to give back and touch lives, we've decided to donate $1,000,000.00 each to five randomly selected individuals, and you have been chosen as one of them.

To confirm and arrange delivery of your gift, please email the CLAIM AGENT (reply to this email) and provide the Claimant Code for verification.

Thank you, and may this blessing bring positive change to your life, as we have been so fortunate to receive ourselves.

Claimant code: KY-PB26/04

Best regards,
Brett Taylor
Claim agent

The Federal Trade Commission (FTC) has issued urgent warnings regarding a surge in task scams and fraudulent job offers targeting people seeking side hustles. These scams often promise high pay for simple, flexible remote work but are designed to steal personal information or money.

Scammers typically advertise through unsolicited texts, emails, or social media messages, often posing as recruiters from well-known companies.

COMMON SIDE HUSTLE SCAMS

Task Scams: Victims are paid small amounts to complete simple online tasks like rating products or "boosting" apps to build trust. They are pressured to deposit their own money, often in cryptocurrency, to unlock higher earnings, which then disappear.

RESHIPPING AND DATA ENTRY SCAMS

These scams offer reshipping packages, which involves stolen goods, or generic data entry roles that require the victim to pay for training or equipment upfront.

FAKE CHECK SCAMS

Scammers send the victim a signing bonus check and ask them to wire back a portion for supplies before the bank discovers the original check is fraudulent.

Red flags to look for are that no legitimate employer will ever ask you to pay for a job, training, or equipment upfront.

Too-good-to-be-true where flexibility and high pay for minimal effort or fast cash.

Urgency and pressure are how scammers often claim a position will disappear if you don't act immediately. They do this so you don't do any research to find out they are scammers.

Vague job descriptions are postings that are nonspecific about actual duties and are often designed to attract as many victims as possible.

Protect yourself by researching the company independently. Look for its official website and contact them directly through verified channels.

Use the company name plus words like scam, review, or complaint in a search engine. Use safe resources such as the FTC Job Scam Portal, and official sites like USAJOBS are reliable places to start your search. Get a second opinion by talking to a friend or family member before accepting an unexpected offer; they may spot a red flag you missed. If you encounter a scam, you should report it immediately at the FTC Fraud Reporting site to help authorities track and stop these operations.

Are you currently evaluating a specific job offer or platform that you would like me to help you verify for potential red flags? AI can make mistakes, so double-check. Many of the scams listed are what I receive and probably many others in their daily emails. A scammer knows he is a scammer, so there is no point in telling him. Your time is valuable. Respect yourself, learn, and move on. Your healing comes first. Do not "play" with scammers. Attention keeps the scam alive. The longer you talk, the more chances they get to lie, guilt you, and pull you back in. They may even try to hack your account and use your profile to scam others.

EMAIL SCAMS

Stacy Barngrover 11:01 AM
To: SupportOffice@mcafe...›
McAfee #164838 Renewal Payment Alert SMS
Invoice Date: Tuesday, March 03, 2026 00:01:38
Transaction ID: FPL-713-YU-5605
Toll-free: +1 (801) 340-2863
Hello again!,

Just a heads-up that your Premium Protection Membership will be automatically renewed in the next 24 hours, with USD 625.41 being debited from your account.

Membership Details:
Start Date: Tuesday, March 03, 2026
Membership ID: FPL-713-YU-5605
Member Name:
Member Email: ladyfarmer1@comcast.net
Membership Duration: 5-Year Lease
Support Plan: McAfee Utilities Ultimate PC Tune-Up
Amount: USD 625.41

For any assistance or changes to your account, please contact us at +1 (801) 340-2863.

With Loving Thanks,
Shawanda Lavalley
McAfee, Inc.
Address: 2702 Horace St., Bennettsville, SC 29512 USA

IRS EMAIL SCAM

US Internal Service
To: ladyfarmer1@comcast... ›
[News] Tax Records Ready for Review
Important Tax Document Posted

A new tax document has been securely uploaded to your online account.

This file reflects recent updates to your federal tax information and may be needed for filing or record-keeping.

You may download the document directly from the link below:

Download Tax Statement

Note: Retain a copy for your files. For more help, visit IRS Help.

Automated message. Please do not reply to this email. Visit IRS.gov for official details. This is a scam email; don't click on any link.

If you get an email, text, letter, or call that claims to be from the IRS, or if you see social media posts about how to get a big refund, it might be a scam or bad tax advice.

An email, call, or message could be a scam if it is unexpected, rushes or threatens you, offers refunds, credits, or deductions, pressures you for personal or financial information, or asks you to pay now or else.

Incorrect information on how to get a bigger refund misleads you to report fake income, federal income tax withholding, and employers on Form W-2, Wage and Tax Statements.

IRS EMAIL SCAM

Re: IRS form delayed - verification required
To the account owner,

This email references documentation for available tax advantages.

Action needed on advantage record TAX-CRD-2025-176972 to maintain benefit entitlement eligibility.

Benefit eligibility documentation is available here: complete documentation

Please ensure forms are completed for benefit access. This message does not require immediate action if forms are current.

Tax Compliance Administration
Tax Form Administrator LLC
dillonmarlene.uk24@gmail.com

URGENT ATTENTION

Dear Beneficiary,

How are you doing? I am Marlene Dillon, my confidence is in you. I need a foreign partner whose name can be used to facilitate the transfer of 7 million euro for our mutual benefit from foreign contracts through my private connections. The funds are presently waiting to be remitted from one of the commercial banks here in the United Kingdom to any overseas beneficiary confirmed by me as an associate. I cannot acquire this money in my name. As a high-placed civil servant, I am not allowed by the civil service code of conduct to own or operate a bank account outside of my shores.

On the other hand, it is not safe for me to keep this money here. What I am requesting from you is to be my silent partner and receive the funds as the sole benefactor to the contract amount, for which I shall secure all legal documentation to authenticate our claim. Receive the funds as the beneficiary, take out your commission, and keep the rest of the money until I arrive there to meet you after the transfer is completed. The fund would be shared as follows: (1) 40% to you as commission for your cooperation and assistance in facilitating the transfer, while 50% belongs to me and my colleague, and 10% will take care of the expenses incurred from the amount in the transaction process.

And you will be free to take out your commission immediately after the money hits your country. Since my objective is to invest the money in a foreign country, the transaction is legitimate, and the money will be transferred successfully with all necessary back-up official documents. As soon as we reach an agreement, immediately respond with:

Your Full Name
Your Occupation
Your Telephone Number
Your Country
Your Home Address

Best Regards,
Marlene Dillon
United Kingdom

Attached finance overview for assessment
+1-(983)-220-3542
9AJGI6-S734EOS0T76

Payment Confirmation PayPal Transaction amount 0.0025 BTC has been processed successfully. ladyfarmer1@comcast.net, thank you for your recent transaction with PayPal. We're pleased to confirm that your order has been successfully completed. We hope your experience meets your expectations. You may view the transaction in your recent activity shortly.

Product Description: Invoice ID: 9AJGI6-S734EQS0T76

Item Name: BTC purchase

Order Date: 01/13/2026 Amount: 434.00 USD Payment Method: Credit Card Auto-Debit. If this transaction was not authorized by you, we kindly ask that you contact our support team within 12 hours to initiate a review and refund process for your membership. You can reach us toll-free at: +1(808)302-5405.

Regards,
Billing Department
Queries & Feedback: +1(983)220-3542 (Toll-Free)

Please do not reply to this message, as it is sent from an unmonitored email address. For assistance, kindly contact customer service at +1-(983)229-3542.

Act Now: Resolve Your Account Issue

Critical Financial Collections Alert—Immediate Action Required

Today's Date: January 12, 2026

Final attempt to resolve your outstanding balance before immediate escalation.

IMMEDIATE REPLY REQUIRED TO PREVENT ENFORCEMENT ACTIVITY

Attention, your outstanding balance with Cash Advance USA has been transferred to Prime Debt Settlement for urgent recovery. Your account is now a seriously past-due delinquent obligation requiring immediate resolution. Continued nonresponse has escalated your case to a critical stage and may result in legal proceedings, wage garnishment, liens, and reporting to national credit bureaus. Failure to reply increases recovery actions, additional fees, and greater long-term financial damage.

Account Summary
Account Number: PDS#20:920573-16
Outstanding Balance: $1,533.24
Original Creditor: Cash Advance America parent for Net Credit, On Stride Financial, Headway

Capital, Rapid Cash, The Money Box, Cash Money, Wage Day Advance, and affiliated lender

Credit Bureau: Experian

Status: Account in Collection—Derogatory

Agency: Prime Debt Settlement

Debt Type: Unsecured Loan

Responsibility: Individual

Nonresponse Consequences

Failure to respond within 3 hours may result in intensified recovery activity, legal review and escalation, updated status with Equifax, and other lawful financial enforcement actions.

Payment Options:

Total balance—$1,533.24

One-time payment: Pay $433.00 today (save $1,100.24)

Biweekly payments: $50 (30 payments), start today

Monthly payments: $150 (10 payments), start today

No terms can be secured until we receive your response.

Immediate response instructions: Click "reply all" to ensure correct routing. Replies not using "reply all" may experience processing delays.

Signature
Sincerely,
Prime Debt Settlement—Recovery Department
Authorized Staff Attorney: KS Bar #289473

This notice includes essential information regarding a financial obligation. If you are not the intended recipient, delete immediately. Failure to respond does not remove the obligation. A reply within 3 hours is strongly advised.

©2025 Prime Debt Settlement | Licensed KS-CA-4829173 FDCPA Compliant

I do not know how many of these I have received and checked all credit bureau reports and nothing. Don't click on "reply all" buttons ever!

CLOUD STORAGE BILLING DEPT.

Notice of Service Termination:
Plan
250 GB Additional Cloud Storage
Status
Suspended
Date
Today

Please update your billing information immediately. Failure to do so will result in the permanent deletion of your archives, photos, and uploaded documents.

Update Billing Info →

Regards,
The Cloud Storage Team

Here is another one I received as well.

UNPROTECTED471985
CLOUD

This season's irreplaceable memories…

Family gatherings. Gift openings. Winter activities.

Each day of the holiday period brings more photos and videos of the people you care about most.

But right now, you are relying solely on a single device.

Storage Protection is Inactive

If your phone breaks or is lost today, your holiday photos are gone forever.

SECURE MY PHOTOS NOW

Last reminder: Important info inside

YOUR STORAGE COULD BE FULL

Action required to avoid data loss

If your storage runs out, new files and emails will be blocked, backups will fail silently, and important data may be lost permanently.

URGENT REMINDER

Your files, photos, and important documents could be at risk.

Upgrade now—failure to act may result in backup suspension. This is a critical system reminder.

Company name:

Street address:

City, country:

Your account has been inactive and is over limit. Per our retention policy, your files are scheduled to be removed. Renew your plan by January 1, 2026, to save your data! Enough already!

Another email scam is "Your Oral-B dental kit awaits!" Dear United Healthcare customer, we are delighted to inform you that you have been selected as one of our valued winners. As a gesture of our appreciation, we are pleased to award you an Oral-B dental kit. Thank you for your continued trust and encouragement. They want you to click a link.

CLAIM YOUR REWARD

Another email scam I receive is telling me the payment for my Netflix subscription was denied and I can update payment information by clicking on the link in the email. Scam! I send a check, and Netflix is included in the cable bill.

Another email just received reads:

> Thank you for choosing HomeServe for your home repair coverage. Please review your service agreement and coverage details by clicking on the button below.
>
> Sincerely,
> REVIEW SERVICE AGREEMENT

More scams to watch out for: getting a phone call from a relief check company. They explain that a relief check for a certain amount is waiting for you to collect. They tell you to search your name and to collect the check before the check is returned. During a two-month time frame, the Better Business Bureau (BBB) had received a little over 800 complaints about this scam. Scams like this lead to identity theft.

With AI getting better and better, it is hard to distinguish if calls, photos, or video chats are legitimate or not. The best thing is to not trust anyone or anything sending any of those to you.

This is what happened to me when I was trying to purchase gift cards as a payment method. I am so glad that this is being done to help people from getting taken advantage of.

A store actually stopped me from sending funds, and if you try to purchase gift cards for certain amounts, the transaction is denied due to it being a scam. They will send a manager over to talk to you about the matter, and it is very embarrassing. If you try to purchase the gift cards at their online store, the transaction is blocked as well. Most of the online cash payment apps are denying transactions as well, claiming scam. The perpetrators want you to process the transactions as friends and family because you will not be able to file a claim for a refund. If you process it as goods and services, they ask you to ask for a refund. It has happened to me. Now, the online cash payment apps are trying to stop these types of scams from taking place.

EMPLOYMENT SCAMS

Due to so many people being laid off, employment scams are on the rise. These unemployed people are so desperate to get a job, they are willing to pay a fee that fraudulent job sites are asking for. Most of the social media and job websites are fraudulent and just want to gain access to your personal information. You are never required to pay to get a job or an interview. Don't believe it if they say you can work for little hours for great pay. Too good to be true. Before doing something you regret, check the company's website to make sure they are hiring and if the person is an actual employee of the company.

DIGITAL SCAMS

These digital scams consist of being contacted by AI video chats, consisting of criminals claiming you are under a criminal investigation and will be arrested. They are portraying police officers or customs officials. They inform you that you are being charged for money laundering or that illegal drugs were intercepted en route to your home. This is all done digitally for hours on top of hours. They transfer you from person to person and show you forged documents in order to extort money from you with threats of being arrested.

You get a text message asking if you are busy or they are running late from an unknown number not in your contacts. If you reply, then they apologize and ask if you are ever in their area you can meet for.

BOGUS DEBT SCAM

You receive a final notice claiming that you have an overdue loan. They will be turning you in to the credit bureau if it is not paid. They give you an option to pay $592.00 now and save $1,000.00 by doing that. Do not pay it nor respond to it. I called the credit bureau they claimed they were turning me in to, and the credit bureau said it was not listed on my report, and they sent me the report. I received emails for being turned in to all three credit bureaus. If it is listed, you may be a victim of identity theft.

GHOST BROKERS

These people are posing as insurance agents who try to sell you bogus insurance policies. An actual insurance agent has a brick-and-mortar office, an easily accessible phone number that can be searched on the internet, and has a license to sell insurance. If in doubt, contact your state's insurance department. They do not pressure you to fill out applications for same-day sales, cheap rates, or won't take any other payments but cash. They are scammers!

I bought a pair of earrings on an online auction site and paid good money for them. They were a marquise-cut diamond in gold. I was given a record of authenticity, only to find out the diamonds were fake when I cashed them in. I tried to contact the seller on the auction site, and they are no longer in business. I even added them to my jewelry insurance. The seller has gone out of business and…

Attaching the paper saying it was a diamond.

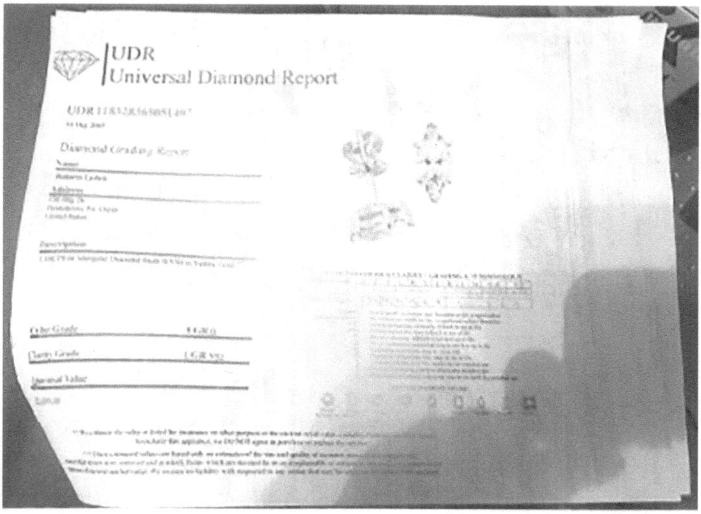

GIFT CARD SCAMS

Fake emergencies, or they impersonate grandkids, bosses, or authority figures, contact you via calls, emails, or texts demanding you to purchase certain gift cards for last-minute gifts or payments. They want you to scratch the back of cards for personal identification numbers or codes. Some give step-by-step directions for you to follow. Once they are given the codes, the cards are drained, and it is now untraceable cash for the scammers.

PARKING METER SCAMS

Scammers put fake QR code stickers on parking meters. These QR stickers lead people to websites that steal payment information or want drivers to swipe their credit cards. Always take your time and examine the QR code stickers to make sure they were not tampered with, or just type the official URLs or use safer apps such as ParkMobile or Passport. Make sure no one is near you when you are close to the parking meter. Try to make sure the QR code is legitimate. If it looks as if it was tampered with, do not scan it. Make sure all is spelled correctly.

PERSONAL LOANS VOICEMAIL

You receive spam calls, and this is the message they leave:

"We offer you all kinds of loans like personal loan, refinance, debt consolidation, medical bills, home renovation, loan on bad credit score. Call us back on 980-250-6335. Press one to repeat again." Delete and report as spam!

Another email scam I received:

> Hi Email Owner,
>
> Can I Trust you with My Donation? I know it will be a great surprise reading from me, but please consider this as a divine intervention as a pastor explained to me. My name is Mrs. Anita Latrice Martin, a widow from Honolulu, Hawaii, USA, and I am writing to you from my sick bed because I have been fighting cancer, and the doctors say I have only a few weeks left. I want to entrust you with my properties and cash in my private account worth $18.5 Million USD in your care for charity purposes to help the less privileged, as my late husband's relatives want me dead so that they will claim all my late husband and I worked for. I will tell you more about myself and what you need to do with the money once you receive it. Please write to me as soon as possible. My health is pretty bad, and my doctors say I will be moved to the hospice care unit any

time soon. Have a blessed day, and please do pray for me. God bless you.

Best Regards,
Mrs. Anita Latrice Martin
E-mail: msanitamartin64@gmail.com:s6425587@ct.ac.th
You have been selected to receive $18.5 Million USD.
Happy New Year.

This is a scam email, and do not reply; delete and block!

I had a scary thing happen last night! Just as I was going to bed, I got a series of emails from PayPal regarding a new PayPal account. Someone tried to set up a new account using the email address that I set up specifically for tour guiding. They used a different name, phone number, and SSN, but my email. Luckily, I caught it before I clicked on "verify your email." I checked the return email, and they were all valid emails from PayPal. I tried logging into that account by trying to change the password, but that's when I noticed the erroneous number, and it told me my SSN was wrong.

IRS SCAM

Criminals also target businesses and payroll companies by email to steal Form W-2 data. They file fraudulent returns in other people's names for refunds.

Scammers use fraudulent Forms W-8BEN to get personal information such as mother's maiden name, passport numbers, PINs, and passcodes. Scammers' messages may claim that anti-money laundering regulations require a review of client information, and they ask you to complete an attached form. A big no-no! You're exempt from tax withholdings on income and tax reporting.

They offer to help you create an IRS account to steal your personal information.

Request gift cards for payments of fake tax bills.

Scammers want to help you file casualty loss claims or get big tax refunds. Impersonators claim to work for or on behalf of the IRS.

Bad tax advice on social media can mislead you about your credit or refund eligibility. Influencers may convince you to lie on tax forms or suggest the IRS is keeping a tax credit secret from you. Social media posts may put you in touch with scammers.

Scammers send a tax bill to trick you into paying them.

Incorrect information on how to get a bigger refund misleads you to claim credits you're not eligible for. This leads to a delayed refund, audit, or other consequences like fines or imprisonment.

Dishonest or uninformed tax preparers misrepresent rules for claiming credits. Aggressive advertising, mail, and online sources mislead you to file an incorrect return. They charge large, upfront fees or a fee based on your refund amount.

IRS impersonators call disaster victims offering to help file a casualty loss claim. We never call without notifying people by mail.

Scammers target people over age 65 or nearing retirement for personal or financial information or money. Often, once you give them money, they ask for more. When scammers trick you to withdraw from your retirement account, it could affect your taxes.

Bad tax advice on social media can mislead you about your credit or refund eligibility. Influencers may convince you to lie on tax forms or suggest the IRS is keeping a tax credit secret from you. Social media posts may put you in touch with scammers.

If box 1 on Form 1099-G, Certain Government Payments, shows unemployment compensation you didn't get, you may be a victim of identity theft. Criminals can use your information to file fake unemployment claims, leaving you with taxable income to report.

If you were scammed, had your information stolen, or suspect fraud, there are actions you can take. Report fraud, scam, or other identity theft immediately!

INTERNET CRIME COMPLAINT CENTER SCAM

Hello Facebook users, due to the increased rate of scams on the internet, the Internet Crime Complaint Center has partnered with Facebook to help victims recover stolen funds and combat scam claims on the internet. If you've been scammed, regardless of when it happened, please contact us directly via Messenger for investigation and potential recovery of stolen funds for free. Thank you. Chat in Messenger. This is a scam!

Yes, the FBI's Internet Crime Complaint Center (IC3) works with reporting cybercrimes that occur on platforms like Facebook, but it doesn't partner directly with Facebook; instead, they encourage victims to report to IC3 (ic3.gov) for federal investigation and to report directly to Facebook for content violations, with both agencies focusing on different aspects of online crime and safety. Law enforcement uses IC3 reports to identify trends and investigate cybercriminals, while Facebook handles user-reported content against its Community Standards.

FAKE JOBS, REAL LOSSES

Jobs are listed on a social media platform or in text messages offering work-from-home jobs. Some of these jobs are data entry, paperwork processing, or clicking a like button on a post or a video to boost a company's online presence. These jobs promise people high paychecks, and no experience is necessary. The downfall to the job is that you might need to pay for equipment needed for your training. They sometimes will tell you they will send a check to cover these expenditures, only to come to find out the check was bogus after you already cashed it. Now you owe that money back. The listing looks so professional, only to find out you were scammed. Always contact the company to make sure that all is legitimate. Do research always before entering into a contract or before cashing a check that reimburses you for equipment.

CLEAR JUSTICE SUPPORT HUB SCAM

This is where they want you to use Clear Justice Support via chat to aid in recovery of lost funds. Do not send them a chat. It is bogus. I found this information for this company: "Reviews for 'Clear Justice Support Hub' are hard to find, but similar services like 'Clear-Record.' This one clears your arrest record." This is most likely a scam because official government and legal entities do not use social media messaging to initiate legal action, ask for money, nor ask for personal information. This aligns with government imposter scams. Do not respond.

The "Clear Justice Support" that you see on Facebook and Marketplace is a scam! They are fake profiles where they try to gain access to your personal information and money. They try to get you to talk to them on a social media app, which they are already on, telling you they can help if you were scammed. It is not worth your while to report to Facebook due to not removing the fraudulent people.

TSB SCAM

This is a scam where criminals are pretending to be representatives from TSB Bank to get your personal banking information. They also try to download malicious software onto your electronic device. They also will try to transfer money to a fake "safe" account by contacting you through texts or emails. They will ask for PINs. Do not give any personal information, such as passwords, one-time security codes, or remote access to your devices. Always check with your bank to see if all is legitimate! Report all! There is actually a person who told their TSB story, and you can google TSB scams to find and read it.

BANK ACCOUNT SCAMS USING PHONE NUMBER

Yes, a scammer can potentially access your bank account using your phone number, primarily through a SIM swap scam, where they trick your mobile carrier into transferring your number to their SIM card, allowing them to intercept two-factor authentication (2FA) codes and password resets. While your number alone isn't enough, it's a key to unlocking accounts, especially if they also have other personal info from data breaches or phishing, enabling them to bypass security and drain funds. They gather personal details (name, address, birthdate) and convince your carrier to port your number to a SIM they control, giving them access to SMS codes. Once they control your number, they intercept SMS codes sent for logging into your bank, email, and social media, and use them to reset passwords. With control of your number and intercepted codes, they can access your bank, drain funds, max out credit cards, or take out loans.

How to protect yourself. Add a PIN or password to your mobile account to prevent unauthorized porting. Switch from SMS-based 2FA to authenticator apps (like Authy) or security keys, which are more secure than text messages. Don't click links or share personal info from unexpected calls, texts, or emails. Use strong, unique passwords and enable 2FA on all accounts. Regularly check bank statements for suspicious activity.

CRYPTO SCAMS

Never call a phone number back that you do not know. This is what can happen.

You can be connected to someone who claims to be a representative from Apple, and they are a scammer. They tell you that you accepted a sale from Russia, and you need to go to the bank and take out your money before Russia empties your bank. The criminals tell you they are going to protect your money by holding it in a secure account. They have you then go to a crypto kiosk and use the money to purchase crypto, and it would be protected until the threat was gone. Do not do that! Over 12,000 complaints were filed with the FBI's Internet Crime Complaint Center (IC3) last year, which marks a "clear and constant rise" in cryptocurrency kiosk scams over recent years. Once money is sent this way, it cannot be reversed. Scammers use a predictable set of scripts—just tailored with different storylines. They might tell you that you might owe money to a utility company, the police, or the IRS. They tell you to avoid being arrested, power shutoffs, or legal trouble, payment is needed immediately. They request you to go to a Bitcoin ATM near you. They will give you a wallet address to send alleged payment to. A fake bank investigator lets you think that your bank account is compromised, and they might ask you to move money out of your account to protect your funds. They will lead you step-by-step on how to take out funds and deposit the funds into a crypto ATM. They also can say that you won something, and taxes need to be paid on your winnings before the prize can be released. They also might say that a relative or grandchild is in trouble. Once again, they want you to send crypto for bail, legal fees, or medical bills. Special deals are being offered at low prices, and the only payment acceptable is crypto at an ATM, and once you send payment, you realize you have been scammed. In nearly all these cases, the scammer gives step-by-step instructions to the victim on the phone, keeping them on the line until the transaction is complete.

Steps to avoid these scams are: If anyone instructs you to use a crypto ATM to pay a fee of any kind, it is a scam. Period. Legitimate companies, government agencies, banks, and law enforcement never demand payment in cryptocurrency, especially through a kiosk or ATM. Crypto ATMs are used only for personal crypto purchases, not payments. To stay safe, hang up. End a call or online conversation immediately if someone pressures you for urgent payment. Never trust caller ID. Scammers can spoof any number, including the police or your bank. End the call and use the phone number on your bank statement, the back of your credit card, or the agency's website to get the real number. Get a reality check. Talk to a trusted relative or friend before sending any money. Scammers rely on creating a sense of urgency and isolation, so you won't realize what's happening. Report incidents. Report a suspected scam call or message to the FTC or your local police. Even partial information can help investigators. Criminals are exploiting the speed and anonymity of Bitcoin ATMs to target unsuspecting people. Awareness is your best defense. Remember, if someone tells you to solve a problem by depositing cash into a crypto ATM, it's not a solution—it's a scam. Stop, hang up, and get help before you lose money you can't get back. You can also share this information with family and friends at holiday gatherings. And if you're inspired to make even more of a difference, the next time you see an ATM machine, let the nearby cashier know what they're often used for. Ask them to keep an eye out for people—often elderly—attempting to deposit money while on their mobile phone.

UBER SCAMS

This might be a new wave of Uber-related scams. You are matched with an Uber driver, and the driver calls and asks for your phone number and code that was sent to your email or text. He claims it is a new Uber policy and needs the information before he could pick you up. Do not give out the information. Uber will never ask for your verification code or any personal information over the phone. If someone does, it's a scam—hang up, cancel, and report the ride immediately.

DELIVERY SCAM

Scammers send out phishing emails and texts that look like they actually come from legitimate companies such as UPS, FedEx, or the US Postal Service. They say that you have missed deliveries or oncoming deliveries and want you to click on links that lead to fraudulent pages that ask for personal information or sites that can be infected with malware.

ONLINE SHOPPING SCAMS

Criminals use fake posts and social media campaigns to sometimes impersonate major brands or tout products they never intend to ship. "We have seen an increase in consumers buying from social media without doing their research. Most social media ads are not vetted," warns Nofziger. "Be careful when you see an item offered at below market price. If you do click on an ad, make sure it directs you to the page you want to be on."

TRAVEL SCAMS

You receive emails or texts offering deals for free flights for you to share personal information such as credit card numbers or click on links that download malware. Be leery of websites also pretending to be legitimate hotels, airlines, and other travel-related businesses.

BRUNT WORKWEAR BAD REVIEW AND SCAM

There have been reports regarding Brunt Workwear claiming issues with product durability and both marketing and customer service. The reports claim that the boots fall apart within a 6-to-12-month period. During this time frame, the soles separate from the boot, materials tear, and waterproofing is not up to par, as well. The company is getting negative reviews on the website and deleting them. Warranty support is bad, misleading, and not being honored to replace the product. The only thing that is being offered is minimal discounts on a new pair, instead of a refund. Also, the company has been targeted with return fraud, which can be customer service issues. Customers say that the boot does not fit properly and the heel cup is uncomfortable and the ankle area is entirely too loose. The company uses aggressive blue-collar-branded social media advertising that customers find misleading compared to the actual product performance.

INVESTMENT SCAMS

Investment-related frauds and scams aren't the most common, but they can be the costliest. Losses reported for fraud were $9,360. The total amount reported to the FTC in total losses was more than $5.84 billion in the year 2024 alone.

Investment-related scams and fraud can happen when you pay for tips, seminars, or courses that promise to teach you how to make money or promise to invest on your behalf. Payments usually asked for can be art, bonds, cryptocurrency, gift cards, gold, wire transfer. They're nontraceable payment methods.

Scammers also can be much more personal, and many romance scams involve investment-related fraud. The scammer grooms the victim, and they might spend weeks or months getting to know you. They are very good at the grooming process and will tell you things that are so believable that you actually see them as the real person whose identity they stole. They will then tell you that their bank account is froze, in trouble with the law, need medical help, and much more to get financial assistance from you, share an investment tip.

In order to protect yourself, never send payments to anyone you don't know, be wary of anyone who tries to entice you with large investment returns, a secret method, insider tips, or promises of passive incomes. If you're intrigued by an investment, the Financial Industry Regulatory Authority (FINRA) has a list of sites and tools that can be used to investigate the investment and the people trying to scam you.

INTERNET RECOVERY SCAMS

Reports related to internet services may cover fraudulent interactions with websites that sell content, online advertisements, online payment services, video games, virtual reality, and social networks. The fraud reports can also stem from internet service providers that mislead consumers about the cost, speed, or access of their service.

Protect yourself by being cautious when interacting with other people online and watch out for online marketplace scams and ads that are sent to you to scam online stores. Make sure to monitor your monthly subscriptions and internet costs.

Mortgage foreclosure relief and debt management has desperate homeowners struggling to keep up with their payments may be the target of mortgage relief scams. This form of fraud may involve false promises to negotiate changes to your loan with your lender in exchange for an upfront fee.

The scammer may say that they're a housing counselor, an attorney, or even a government representative. They may also offer to buy your home to help you get back on your feet or help you get a deal on a rescue loan.

They'll advise you not to speak with your lender, attorney, or other professional, and they may ask you to make your mortgage payment directly to them. But once they have your money, they vanish into thin air.

It's illegal for a debt relief company or service to charge you a fee for mortgage assistance or relief until you receive and accept a written loan modification offer from your lender. If an individual or service tries to charge you anything before that point, it's a scam, and don't fall for it.

If you're having trouble with your mortgage payment, reach out to your lender or loan servicer to talk about relief options. It is also beneficial to work with a housing counselor. You can find legitimate housing counselors through the US Department of Housing and Urban Development.

If you believe you might have been scammed, you will need to hire an attorney to represent you. Take your time to research and evaluate local options. Ask friends and family members for recommendations, and be sure to verify that they're licensed in your state and have good customer reviews.

Report the scam or fraud to the FTC on ReportFraud.ftc.gov. If you think your personal information was stolen, you can also file an identity theft report on IdentityTheft.gov. In either case, the FTC will share some next steps you can take to protect yourself or recover your identity.

Change all passwords and use multi-factor authentication (MFA) or passkeys. Add a freeze or fraud alert to the three credit bureaus.

SCAMS IMPERSONATING DACHENG LAW OFFICE

Scammers are creating fake websites, using fraudulent email domains, and stealing attorney identities to deceive clients, particularly in high-value, cross-border, or cryptocurrency transactions. These scams often involve redirecting payment instructions or promising to recover lost assets to defraud victims of money.

Scammers have created websites using the names and photographs of partners from reputable firms, such as the case with the Hong Kong Law Society alerting the public of a fake entity pretending to be solicitors.

Scammers will also monitor or initiate email communication requesting urgent funds via telegraphic transfer, often using slightly altered email domains to impersonate real staff.

Fraudulent entities, mostly on social media, falsely claim to be connected to the Dacheng Law Firm or other reputable firms, promising to recover lost cryptocurrency assets as a way to lure victims into paying upfront fees, which are scams.

Due to the split between Dentons and Beijing Dacheng in 2023, they heightened security, data, and regulatory. The challenges in China made it easier for malicious actors to exploit confusion regarding the relationship between the two entities.

Protect yourself by always verifying the authenticity of a solicitor or law firm through official, independent sources like the local Law Society or Bar Association, check domain names, and verify all payment methods.

FBI SCAMS

The FBI investigates and disrupts complex financial crimes, including cybercrime, tech support scams, and government impersonation scams. We work with partners to stay ahead of emerging threats and educate the public on recognizing and reporting suspicious activity. Our goal is to protect individuals, businesses, and communities from financial harm. Scammers are impersonating FBI Internet Crime Complaint Center (IC3) employees on Facebook to target previous scam victims with recovery scams, according to the FBI and IC3. These fraudsters use fake profiles, often joining support groups for scam victims, to solicit money or personal information under the guise of recovering lost funds. Victims of previous online scams are contacted via Facebook Messenger, WhatsApp, or other social media, often by profiles posing as women. Scammers claim they can recover previously lost money or cryptocurrency. They may direct users to contact a chief director or agent, such as Jaime Quin. They will ask for sensitive personal data or upfront fees to initiate the recovery process. Remember, the real IC3 will not reach out via social media, text, or email, nor will they call you directly to ask for money or personal details. The government will not ask for payment to recover stolen assets. If you believe you are being targeted, do not engage. Report the contact directly at www.ic3.gov. Scammers often move conversations to encrypted apps like Telegram to avoid detection.

If you are contacted by someone claiming to be from the FBI or IC3 on Facebook, it is a scam.

NEW RULE MAY ADD TO THE OF TAX SEASON IRS IMPOSTOR

Impostor scams surge during tax season, and a new rule about how refunds are issued can cause confusion and stress. As of this year, the IRS will only distribute tax refunds electronically as the federal government moves away from paper checks. It is change like this that provides more opportunities for scammers to impersonate the agency.

How to help protect yourself is to know that if you ever receive an unexpected communication that claims to be from the IRS, it is a scam. They only send letters! They may say you owe back taxes and face legal action if you don't act fast and pay immediately, or they may ask for banking details to update refund information because of the new rule. They may ask for payments by wire transfer, cryptocurrency, or by purchasing gift cards and sharing the numbers off the back. They might tell you that you have a refund coming or even a tax rebate, which you can claim by clicking a link or calling a phone number. Do not click on the link or call the phone number. Generally, the IRS will first send a letter through the mail before the agency otherwise contacts taxpayers; it only uses email and text with your permission.

Federal agencies never request payment via wire transfer, cryptocurrency, or gift card. In 100 percent of these scenarios, it is a scam.

If a tax filer does not include direct deposit information on their 2025 return, the IRS will send a letter to the last known address to request bank information or to find out why the taxpayer cannot provide it.

If you get a call claiming to be from the IRS, hang up or, better yet, don't pick up the call to begin with.

If you want to confirm your tax payment status, call the IRS directly using a trusted number from an official letter, at IRS.gov, or log into your IRS Online Account if you have one.

Beyond IRS impostors, tax ID fraud is also a concern. Consider obtaining an IRS identity protection PIN. The PIN is known only to you and the IRS, and your return cannot be processed without it.

PLATFORMS WON'T TAKE DOWN IMPOSTORS PROFILES

Some have been there, not all. You come across a profile on social media that you know is fake, and you take the time to report the profile, only to get a response minutes later. The response from the platform is that the profile does not violate the platform's community standards. It is getting out of hand and very frustrating. The reason is because social media platforms use artificial intelligence (AI) to review the majority of the millions of reports received each and every day. This is the reason they are unable to spot the subtle nuances of a scammer profile.

The lack of action from online platforms to take down fraudulent profiles causes undeniable financial and emotional harm to countless cybercrime victims each year. If romance scams and crypto fraud are such a huge problem, why aren't platforms doing more about the scams? Also, what role does Section 230 play in the scams taking place on the platforms?

This isn't just a few fraudulent profiles lost in the shuffle; it is a bigger issue. Among romance scam groups, their participants said that 80 percent met their scammers on a social media or dating platform.

Here are some reasons why there are so many fraudulent accounts that go undetected.

Social media and dating platforms manage billions of accounts. To keep up with all of the accounts, they rely heavily on automated moderation. These systems are built to flag clear violations but struggle to find the slow, relationship-building nature of romance and crypto investment fraud.

Scammers are professionals at avoiding these automated detection systems. To an algorithm, these fake profiles are almost identical to genuine ones.

In reporting a profile, you're limited to a few checkboxes or short text fields. Full conversation histories, patterns of manipulation, and escalating pressure aren't visible to reviewers.

Platforms prioritize the detection of issues such as violence, extremism, and copyright infringement. Even though it causes substantial financial and emotional harm, fraud ranks below these other issues.

Platforms put the responsibility of finding and reporting these fake profiles solely on their users, and the victims must deal with the platforms' reporting systems while they are coping with grief, shock, and shame. Until platforms are incentivized properly, the burden will always remain on the users.

Congress only added Section 230 to the US Communications Act in 1996. Under Section 230, platforms are protected from being treated as the publisher of user-generated content. This type of protection helped build the modern internet. This means that online platforms, like social media, search engines, and forums, can't be held responsible when users post harmful content. When legal risk is low and tied to user content, heavy investments in fraud detection and safety infrastructure compete with and often lose to revenue-driving features. If we want better outcomes for victims, incentives must be realigned so that the platform's success is not decoupled from user protection. The current misalignment helps explain why, even when harm is widespread and well documented, investment in fraud prevention remains inconsistent.

Platforms like to treat fraud as something that happens to users rather than a risk created by the platform's design. This shifts the responsibility from the platforms to the individuals.

Most platforms are optimized for growth and engagement and would like more user interactions to increase the time spent on their platform. Due to this reason, safety features can add friction or reduce engagement and lose out to features that drive scale and revenue.

Effective fraud detection is a nonstop investment in technology, staffing, and human review for platforms. Scammers adapt quickly, which means safety systems must evolve quickly too. Scam prevention has no clear endpoint and no return on investment.

Online scams operate across borders and jurisdictions, which makes responsibility and enforcement inconsistent. For this reason, no single platform fully owns the problem.

A lot of people's reaction was to repeal Section 230, but that could lead to unintended consequences.

Platforms will likely face massive legal risks for anything and everything posted by their users if Section 230 goes away. To avoid lawsuits, the platforms may remove content more aggressively, even if it's helpful information that is essential for fraud support communities.

Platforms could scale back or eliminate interactive features that make moderation complex. Tools like messaging, groups, or forums help connect people and allow peer-to-peer support, but they could disappear because the legal liability becomes too high.

Larger online platforms can handle higher legal costs, but smaller ones might be forced to get rid of features or shut down completely.

Instead of removing legal protections entirely, a framework could hold platforms accountable while keeping the online environment safe for survivors.

Platforms would retain certain protections only if they actively meet safety obligations. This approach encourages companies to prevent fraud and abuse while keeping supportive community spaces intact.

Platforms have to investigate and take action against all credible reports, especially repeat offenders and known scam networks, instead of relying on users to report the same fraudulent profile over and over again.

Platforms need to publicly share response times, takedown rates, and repeat offender activity. This transparency would create accountability and give users confidence that their reports are being taken seriously.

Reporting tools should be trauma-informed and allow survivors to provide full context. This ensures victims can safely share experiences without being reduced to checkboxes or automated filters.

Romance fraud and crypto investment fraud are predictable crimes occurring in systems designed to connect us. Right now, online fraud victims are absorbing financial devastation, emotional trauma, and long-term instability while platforms operate with little fear of legal repercussions. We don't need to completely repeal Section 230; we need to modernize the incentive structure.

Victims aren't asking to break the internet; they want it fixed. They're asking for a system that stops protecting inaction more than it protects people.

ALBATROSS AMERICA INC. SCAM

Albatross America, Inc., is a Pasadena, California-based third-party logistics provider and importer. They were registered in 2021. They manage shipping for e-commerce and inventory that is imported from China. They have been linked to unsolicited brushing scams. These scams are where customers receive a package that was never ordered by them. The items received are junk, and fake positive reviews are posted.

Albatross America manages the movement of goods and customs clearances. They are registered in Florida and also listed in California. They have strong ties to Zhejiang Albatross International TR. Many users have reported receiving small, unexpected items such as jewelry and phone accessories from the company. If you receive an unordered package, you can keep it and not have to pay, or you can throw it away. This is the type of scam this company does.

REPORTING SCAMS

ssa.gov/scam

Report Social Security–related issues to SSA OIG (oig.ssa.gov/report).

Reporting to the FTC (reportfraud.ftc.gov).

If you believe you have encountered a scammer or fallen victim to one, STOP talking to them immediately, report the profile to the platform; sometimes it helps, others it does not. Gather all (messages, transaction details, profile links).

The most important thing to do is to report the incident to local authorities and consumer protection agencies. In the US, you can report to the FTC or the FBI's Internet Crime Complaint Center (IC3).

In NZ, you can report to NZ Police or Netsafe. In Australia, report to Scamwatch.

Resources

The Authors Guild: https://authorsguild.org/resource/avoiding-publishing-scams

Better Business Bureau: https://www.bbb.org

http://www.scamicide.com

FBI's Internet Crime Complaint Center (IC3): https://www.ic3.gov

Federal Trade Commission: https://reportfraud.ftc.gov

Manhattan District Attorney: https://manhattanda.org/victim-resources/financial-crimes

State Attorneys General: https://www.usa.gov/state-attorney-general

Writer Beware: https://writerbeware.blog/

Resources
(Outside of United States)

Australia: https://www.scamwatch.gov.au/report-a-scam
Canada: https://antifraudcentre-centreantifraude.ca/report-signalez-eng.htm
India: https://cybercrime.gov.in
UK: https://www.actionfraud.police.uk

ftc.gov/calls
Veterans Benefits Administration (.gov)
https://attorneygeneral.gov
Bitdefender Scamio
https://www.pymnts.com/author/pymnts/
ncoa.org
mtlebanon.org
facebook.com
Veterans Benefits Administration (.gov)
idwatchdog.com
Albatross America, Inc.
Veterans Benefits Administration (.gov)

REFERENCES

All of the searches that I have done for research on the various types of scams to be weary of were found on:

https://www.google.com or https://www.safari.com
https://www.apple.com
https://www.fedex.com
https://www.usps.gov
https://www.dhl.com
https://angieslist.com
https://www.truecaller.com
https://www.fastpeoplecheck.com
https://www.numlookup.com
https://www.universalproperty.com
https://www.donotcall.gov
https://www.Duquesnelight.com
https://www.aarp.com
https://www.checkpeople.com
https://www.facebook.com
https://www.messenger.com
https://www.chat.google.com
https://www.tinder.com
https://www.craigslist.com
https://www.ebay.com
https://www.temu.com
https://www.amazon.com
https://www.paypal.com
https://www.cashapp.com
https://www.socialcatfish.com

https://www.linkedin.com
https://www.freecarrierlookup.com
https://www.meta.com
https://www.whitepages.com
https://www.instragram.com
https://home.treasury.gov
https://www.snap.gov
https://www.whispr.com
https://www.dachenglaw.com
https://www.teams.microsoft.com
https://www.whatsapp.com
https://www.telegram.org
https://www.zelle.com
https://www.venmo.com
https://www.pa.gov
https://www.robinhood.com
https://www.indianacountypa.gov

ABOUT THE AUTHOR

Roberta Lydick is a retired elementary school employee from Western Pennsylvania who has dedicated herself to educating others about the growing threat of scams and online fraud. Throughout the years, she became increasingly concerned about the number of people losing money, identities, and confidence after being targeted by scammers and impostors.

Motivated by a desire to help others protect themselves, Roberta began researching common scam tactics and sharing practical information designed to increase awareness and prevention. Her work focuses on helping readers recognize warning signs, understand how scammers operate, and learn effective steps to safeguard their personal information and finances.

Through her books, Roberta strives to empower readers with knowledge, vigilance, and confidence so they can navigate today's increasingly complex digital world with greater security and peace of mind.

www.ingramcontent.com/pod-product-compliance
Lightning Source LLC
LaVergne TN
LVHW100147061126
851857LV00010B/282
9798896016427